THE UPSTART GUIDE TO
OWNING AND MANAGING A DESKTOP PUBLISHING SERVICE

THE UPSTART GUIDE TO
Owning and Managing a Desktop Publishing Service

Dan Ramsey

UPSTART PUBLISHING COMPANY
Chicago, Illinois

Published by Upstart Publishing Company
A Division of Dearborn Publishing Group, Inc.
155 North Wacker Drive
Chicago. Illinois 60606-1719
(800) 235-8866 or (312) 836-4400

Copyright © 1995 by Dan Ramsey
All rights reserved. No part of this work may be reproduced or transmitted in any form or by any means without express written consent of the publisher.

Neither the author nor the publisher of this book is engaged in rendering, by the sale of this book, legal, accounting, or other professional services. The reader is encouraged to employ the services of a competent professional in such matters.

All brand and product names mentioned in this book are copyright, trademarks or registered trademarks/tradenames of their respective owners. Names, addresses, telephone numbers, and related information are included in this book for the convenience of the reader and were current when this book was written. No endorsement is implied.

Library of Congress Cataloging-in-Publication Data
Ramsey, Dan, 1945-
    The upstart guide to owning and managing a desktop publishing service / Dan Ramsey.
        p.   cm.
    Includes index.
    ISBN 0-936894-68-7
    1. Desktop publishing industry—United States—Management. I. Title.
Z244.6.U5R36 1995
070.5'068—dc20   94-22788
                                                                                                                                                                            CIP

Cover design by Paul Perlow Design, New York, NY.

Printed in the United States of America
10 9 8 7 6 5 4 3 2

For a complete catalog of Upstart's small business publications, call (800) 235-8866.

For our good friends, Rob and Shelby Pearson

Contents

Preface *xi*
Acknowledgments *xiii*

1 Opportunities for Desktop Publishing Services 1
Meet Quality Impressions 2
What a Desktop Publishing Service Does 3
Typical Business Day for a Desktop Publishing Service 5
The Market for Desktop Publishing Services 6
The Future of Desktop Publishing Services 7
How Desktop Documents are Produced 7
Life as a Desktop Publisher 8
Income and Profit Potentials 9
Do You Really Want to Start a Business? 12
Action Guidelines 14

2 Requirements for Desktop Publishing Services 15
Assessing Your Personal Goals 16
Assessing Your Personal Values 16
Assessing Your Financial Goals 18
Assessing Your Risk Tolerance 19
Desktop Publishing Tools 19
Desktop Publishing Supplies 38
Calculating Your Business' Financial Requirements 38
Action Guidelines 41

3 Desktop Publishing Service Resources 43
Analyzing Your Own Experiences
    with Printed Documents 43
Determining Customers' Needs 44
Trade Associations for Desktop Publishers 45
Conventions and Seminars for Desktop Publishers 46
Valuable Training Courses for Desktop Publishers 46

Books for Desktop Publishers *47*
Magazines and Trade Journals for Desktop Publishers *48*
Considering a Franchise *49*
Sources for Desktop Publishing Papers *50*
Desktop Publishing Product Suppliers *51*
Small Business Administration Resources *51*
Tax Information Resources *53*
Action Guidelines *55*

4 **Starting Up Your Desktop Publishing Service** *57*
How to Plan for Your Desktop
    Publishing Service's Success *58*
How to Select Your Business Name *59*
Where to Locate Your Business *61*
Selecting the Right Location *64*
Checking Zoning Laws *65*
Understanding Employment Laws *66*
Selecting the Right Business Form *67*
Hiring an Attorney *73*
Hiring an Accountant *74*
Hiring an Insurance Agent *77*
Action Guidelines *78*

5 **Operating Your Desktop Publishing Service** *79*
How to Estimate Operating Costs *79*
How to Establish an Operating Budget *81*
How to Keep Good Records *83*
Understanding Record Systems *86*
Understanding Assets, Liabilities, and Net Worth *88*
Understanding Cash and Accrual Accounting *88*
Managing Accounts Receivable *89*
Managing Payroll Records *90*
Managing Petty Cash *91*
Managing Equipment Records *91*
Pricing Your Desktop Publishing Services *92*

  Selling the Value of Your Services *97*
  Managing Desktop Publishing Tasks *99*
  Managing Time *100*
  Hiring Good Employees *104*
  Understanding and Paying Taxes *105*
  Action Guidelines *109*

6 Marketing Your Desktop Publishing Service *111*
  Understanding Marketing *111*
  How to Market Your Desktop Publishing Services *114*
  Understanding Your Customers *114*
  Finding Prospects *116*
  Selling Desktop Publishing Services *117*
  Establishing an Advertising Program *118*
  Free Advertising and Publicity *122*
  Using Newspaper Advertising *125*
  Using Yellow Pages Advertising *126*
  How to Build Repeat Business *128*
  How to Earn Referral Business *129*
  Action Guidelines *131*

**7 The Financial Side of Your
   Desktop Publishing Service** *133*
  Managing Your Money *134*
  Income Statements *136*
  Balance Sheets *137*
  Cash Flow Forecasts *137*
  Improving Cash Flow *141*
  Building Your Business's Credit *142*
  Getting a Loan *143*
  Managing Interest Rates *146*
  SBA Guaranteed Loans *147*
  How to Offer Credit to Your Customers *149*
  How to Improve Financial Planning *149*
  Action Guidelines *153*

8 Succeeding as a Desktop Publishing Service *155*
   How to Solve Common Business Problems *155*
   How to Profitably Manage Employees *161*
   How to Hire Temporary Help *167*
   The Risks of Business *169*
   How to Survive Business Cycles *174*
   An Eye to the Future *180*
   Planning to Retire *186*
   Action Guidelines *187*

Resources for Small Business *189*
Index *197*

PREFACE

Computers have changed the face of publishing. Typesetting equipment costing hundreds of thousands of dollars has been replaced by computers, laser printers, and software available for less than $10,000. Today, computer-aided or desktop publishing services can prepare brochures, letterheads, business cards, personalized mass mailings, newsletters, signs—even books and magazines—at a fraction of the cost of larger systems. Desktop publishing is now a multimillion dollar industry with numerous opportunities for people who enjoy seeing their work in print.

Desktop publishing can offer you the "freedom of the press." With an understanding of computers and graphics, you can turn your skills into a profitable desktop publishing service. And, if you have more desire than knowledge, there are abundant resources for learning the skills you'll need to succeed as a desktop publisher.

It's the American dream. Fifty-seven percent of all Americans—and almost two-thirds of those under 30—would rather own their own business than work for someone else. Yet Dun & Bradstreet reports that 28 percent of all new businesses fail within the first three years and 63 percent fail within six years. It can also be the American nightmare!

The American reality is that, to arrive at your intended destination, you need a guide—whether you're traveling the road to Timbuktu or the road to small business success. A guide is someone who has traveled that road before and knows where the treasures and dangers are found.

In business, it's not what you know but what you *don't* know that can reduce your chances of success. So success comes from discovering what it is that you don't know about your chosen business opportunity and learning it. Maybe it's a lack of management experience, or financial background, or technical knowledge, or money. Or maybe it's a little bit of each of these.

The Upstart Guide to Owning and Managing a Desktop Publishing Service is a comprehensive book based on my experience as a desktop publisher and author. I have produced a variety of documents from brochures to books using desktop publishing systems. Using a PC, desktop publishing software, and a laser printer, I've published a book on whirligigs, newsletters for industrial clients, brochures for various businesses, and software manuals.

The Upstart Guide to Owning and Managing a Desktop Publishing Service will guide you through the proven steps to starting and operating a successful desktop publishing service. It includes detailed examples from successful desktop publishers. Business and trade terms are defined in context. Specific resources with addresses and phone numbers are included as they relate to the topic. Each chapter ends with *Action Guidelines*, a list of actions to reach your business goals.

The Upstart Guide to Owning and Managing a Desktop Publishing Service includes charts, worksheets, and examples to help you get started faster and to arrive sooner. It will show you how to set prices, build business, pay taxes, and enjoy what you do.

A successful desktop publishing service can be helpful to others and profitable to you. *The Upstart Guide to Owning and Managing a Desktop Publishing Service* will help you do both.

ACKNOWLEDGMENTS

An author is the leader of a team. This book is a team effort that the author managed. Thanks to many people who contributed to the development of this book. They include Barry Harrigan and Annie Rice of the National Association of Desktop Publishers; Robert C. Brenner of Brenner Information Group; Frank Fox of the National Association of Secretarial Services; Linda Simpson of Lin Media Services; Randy Busch of Delrina Technology Inc.; Judy Ramsey of Communication Solutions; Spencer Smith of Upstart Publishing; David H. Bangs, Jr., author of *The Business Planning Guide*; Lori Capps and Roy L. Fietz of the Business Development Center at Southwest Oregon Community College; and The Small Business Administration Office of Business Development.

The author and publisher have used their best efforts in preparing this book, but make no warranty, expressed or implied, regarding the instructions and suggestions contained in it.

OPPORTUNITIES FOR DESKTOP PUBLISHING SERVICES

Desktop publishing (DTP) is one of the fastest growing service businesses in the world. Why? Because new technologies offer businesses the three most important benefits: better, faster, and cheaper.

This book was written and produced using the tools of desktop publishing, as was your favorite magazine, your local newspaper, and a wide variety of other printed products you use every day. Desktop publishing has revolutionized printed communications—and will continue to do so for many years to come.

Desktop publishing is not a get-rich-quick scheme. It simply puts tools and knowledge formerly held by graphic artists and typesetters into the hands of more people. Certainly, some of these hands don't use the tools well, producing graphic chaos. But, for many, the tools can be managed to produce creative and useful documents that better inform or entertain the reader. Desktop publishing services produce informative brochures, easy-to-read instructions, attractive business cards and letterheads, creative advertisements, powerful presentations, and many other valuable documents.

Desktop publishing services also offer business opportunities for those who want to apply skill, hard work, and vision to their daily life. Let's meet one of them.

Meet Quality Impressions

Quality Impressions, Inc., is a successful desktop publishing service in the Midwest. It opened six years ago, producing a variety of documents for businesses and consumers. As competition grew, Quality Impressions focused on its most profitable market: promotional documents for established businesses in its growing metropolitan area. It is also working with a local writer to publish customer newsletters for independent banks across the nation.

Quality Impressions is operated by a family-owned S corporation whose principals are Bonnie and Jack Wilson. Bonnie started the business as a proprietorship and, when it grew, Jack joined in the daily operations and they incorporated. Bonnie has an art degree and Jack a business degree, so she designs and produces the products while he handles sales and records. They recently hired their oldest daughter to help with production.

Quality Impressions started in the Wilson home then moved to a nearby shopping center. After three years there, the Wilsons decided that business gained from the location wasn't sufficient to warrant the high rents. They moved the business back home and Jack makes sales calls at the clients' offices.

Quality Impressions specializes in publishing quality brochures and presentation documents for businesses. It has more than 30 regular clients who ask for presentations and proposals for sales meetings and related needs. Using computer technology, the the Wilsons download the rough proposal from the client using a modem or the fax machine. Their hourly rate is $45. To this they add the cost of special papers and materials. A typical proposal will require six hours of production and about $25 in materials for five copies. They used to bill the client a flat $295 for this service. But the many variables to proposal publishing lost them either money or clients. Now they bill this service by the hour, but will give an estimated cost based on answers to questions they ask the client.

Publishing business plans for clients wanting to start a business led them to working with bankers. In a lunch conversation, Jack learned that a local bank manager wanted a newsletter to keep larger depositors informed of the bank's investment opportunities. Quality Impressions bid and got the job, then found a local writer to develop articles for the newsletter. Now, with that writer, Quality Impressions produces newsletters for other noncompeting banks. By establishing a production system and using computer technology, Quality Impressions now publishes a quarterly banking newsletter that is customized for each of eight banks.

The Wilsons enjoy what they do, appreciate working together, and delight in helping others with their desktop publishing service.

What a Desktop Publishing Service Does

A desktop publishing service uses computers and software to design, typeset, and prepare for printing a variety of documents. Desktop publishing is also referred to as computer-aided publishing, or CAP. Desktop publishing services are found in metropolitan areas as well as in towns of 5,000.

There are three types of desktop publishers: those who publish for others, those who publish for themselves, and those who do both. Most desktop publishing services start by publishing for others. Then, as the owners' skills and understanding of the local market grow, they may see an opportunity for a local or regional publication, such as a local guide book, an advertising publication, or a regional magazine. Because this is a book on how to start your desktop publishing service, it will concentrate on opportunities for those new in business. However, be watchful of other publishing opportunities that can bring you additional profits and promote your primary business, desktop publishing services. Thomas Williams' book, *How to Make $100,000 a Year in Desktop Publishing* (Betterway Publications), outlines ten profitable publishing opportunities.

A desktop publishing service typically offers a wide variety of products and services. It may produce business cards, flyers, brochures, newsletters, advertising, presentations, technical manuals, catalogs, résumés, business plans, reports, employee manuals, and directories for others (Figure 1.1). It may also publish local tourism guides, real estate guides, apartment guides, shopping guides, advertising papers, local history books, newspapers, or other commercial publications for itself or others.

Desktop publishing services that face significant competition often specialize in one or two types of documents, such as

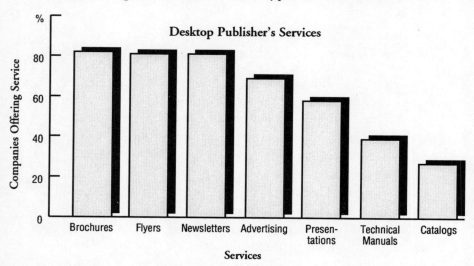

Figure 1.1: Desktop publishers produce a variety of publications. From the *NADTP Journal* study.

brochures or newsletters. In fact, rather than market themselves as a desktop publishing service, they focus their marketing efforts on the specialty. They may call themselves ABC Brochures or ABC Newsletter Service. Of course, they first analyze the market for these specialized services to ensure that it will support them.

In this book, you'll learn about market research as well as how to set up and operate your own desktop publishing service. You'll learn techniques from successful desktop publishers. You'll also learn how to enjoy what you do as well as how to keep on doing it.

Typical Business Day for a Desktop Publishing Service

Since Quality Impressions, Inc. is located in the Wilson home, it doesn't have typical office hours. An answering system with voice mail helps the Wilsons set their own hours. Prospects and customers call their 800 number and are asked to leave a message. Actually, Bonnie hears all incoming messages as they are recorded and can pick up the phone to respond if she wishes. This system allows Bonnie to reduce interruptions to work without missing important calls. Jack is in and out of the office much of the day, selling to clients, and picking up copy and supplies.

Even with the unset office hours, the Wilsons put in a minimum of 10 hours a day each. Bonnie may start in very early in the morning, quit for an hour to help their young children get breakfast and off to school, then return to work. Later in the afternoon, when Jack has most of his sales calls done for the day, he returns to help with the family dinner and assist with production. During the summer, the Wilsons have their children at home all day. If business gets hectic, they have an on-call baby-sitter, who will come over and help with the children. This arrangement works well for the Wilsons and has allowed Quality Impressions to earn more than $130,000 in gross sales in a recent year.

The Market for Desktop Publishing Services

Who will hire you for desktop publishing? Many businesses and individuals will. Businesses need product literature, sales documents, technical documents, and other services. Individuals need résumés, reports, etc. Most of your business will be done with other businesses. Chapter 6 will help you define and reach your market.

For example, one successful desktop publisher developed and sold a New Business Set to people who purchased a business license at the county courthouse. Once a week, she picked up a list of new business names, owners, and addresses, then sent each one a sample packet with pricing. Her New Business Set included 500 business cards, 100 letterheads, 75 brochures, 100 bordered single-page announcements, 200 envelopes, 120 mailing labels, and 200 announcement postcards. Supplies for this package can be purchased for less than $150 from paper suppliers listed in Chapter 3. If the client furnishes the copy or text information, her desktop publishing service offers this new business package for $400 to $600.

Other desktop publishing services offer a Client Presentation package that includes a typeset proposal in a personalized folder and envelope.

One successful desktop publishing service works with a local business consultant to develop and publish business plans for presentation to bankers and venture capital firms.

Another successful desktop publisher specializes in producing and mailing newsletters for medical and professional offices.

The Future of Desktop Publishing Services

Desktop publishing is a product of recent advances in computer and printing technologies. Will desktop publishing survive the next technology breakthrough? Probably. Most important, a desktop publisher who keeps current on the latest technologies of the industry and learns how to creatively apply them will survive. That doesn't mean your business has to be on the leading edge of technology, but you do have to know what technology is valuable to your business and what is not.

Even if, someday, business becomes paperless, desktop publishers will have their expertise in the tools that format data into useful and easy-to-read electronic files. Creative desktop publishers will continue to be in demand.

How Desktop Documents are Produced

All products and services are developed through a process. The process of making a hamburger, for example, requires knowledge (how to prepare), materials (meat, bun, special sauce, etc.), and labor (cooking, assembling, packaging), and results in a specific output (a hamburger) in a form that the customer wants.

There is a process to producing desktop documents. Understanding the mechanics of the process—the required knowledge, materials, labor, and expected results—will make you a better and more efficient desktop publisher.

The knowledge required for producing desktop documents includes written communication skills, an understanding of computers and peripherals, a knowledge of how documents are printed, fundamentals of business and economics, and an understanding of how business does business.

The materials you will need for producing desktop documents include a computer and monitor, printer, software, an office or work area, a telephone, and paper and supplies.

Of course, your desktop publishing service will require labor. It may be your labor designing brochures or it may be the labor of a typesetter, an independent contractor, or a supplier such as a printer. In each case, you must understand what the labor requirements of the process are in order to ensure that the job is being done properly and efficiently.

Finally, you need to define the end result you want, which is actually not the final step, but the first one. Until you understand exactly what your client requires, you cannot define the other elements in your process—knowledge, materials, and labor.

For example, if your service's primary product is client newsletters, your knowledge, materials, and labor are different than if you are publishing your own booklets. In our earlier example, you don't select beef as a material until you've decided that a hamburger is the output or end result you want. You can't make hamburgers using tofu.

All this may sound quite elementary. It is. But it is where more new businesses get lost than anywhere else. They start out with the wrong knowledge, materials, and labor for their clients needs. They look at their solution before they've even discovered what the client's problem is. They start at the wrong end of the process. This book will help you define your client's problem and show you how to solve it with a proven process.

Life as a Desktop Publisher

What can you expect your life to be like if you decide to become a professional desktop publisher? That depends. If you're a square peg trying to fit into a round hole, you will be uncomfortable. If you don't enjoy working with computers and documents and using your skills to help people, you will probably be miserable. If you're looking for a way to get rich quick, try another line of work—one I haven't discovered yet. But if you enjoy helping other people, you have good communication and artistic skills or a strong desire to develop them, experience in the printing or publishing industry, and the need to be an independent business person, producing desktop documents may be a rewarding way of making a living.

If you are an artist or designer first and foremost, you will find that producing desktop documents offers you many opportunities. You will be able to develop your design skills. You will work directly with your client—a satisfying option that most artists don't have. Best of all, you will be paid for your artistic skills. Eventually, you may be able to branch out to other types of art or design work that are more enjoyable and better use your creative skills. Meantime, you will be earning a good living by offering a valuable service to others.

Income and Profit Potentials

How much can you expect to make operating a desktop document production service? Of course, much depends on local need, competition, your skills, and other factors. But there are some guidelines that will get you started.

First, the typical desktop publishing service operated by the owner without employees can sell about $60,000 to $80,000 in services in a year, depending on competition and market conditions. That's earning a rate of $30 to $40 an hour, eight hours a day, five days a week. Few desktop publishing services start out the first year making that much, but most can do so by the second full year of operation.

How much profit should you expect to make? As a service business, much of your income will go to pay for labor. In a one-person office, that's you. Refer to Figure 1.2. Ideally, salary will be approximately 50 percent of income. That's $30,000 to $40,000 in salary for a typical, established firm. Overhead expenses (rent, telephone, advertising, equipment) will take about 30 percent of your income. Direct expenses (document paper, envelopes, printer supplies, etc.) will typi-

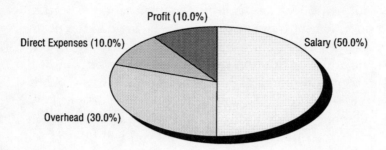

Figure 1.2: Approximate expenses and profits during your second year of operation.

cally take 10 percent of your income. What's left over is profit—about 10 percent of income. Taxes come from this figure before you can call it net profit.

The above figures are for your second year of operation, when you've built repeat and referral business, have developed a target market, and have purchased your equipment and supplies. Your first year will be more difficult as you build your business. Refer to Figure 1.3. During the first year, expect about 75 percent of your estimated second-year revenue and overhead as high as 40 percent of your second-year revenue estimate. That is, if you estimate that second-year sales will total $72,000, estimate first-year sales to be 75 percent of that, or about $54,000. Your salary will be about $21,600 (40%), overhead will be approximately $21,600 (40%), direct expenses of about $5,400 (10%), and profit before taxes of about $5,400 (10%) or about $0 after taxes. Don't plan on getting rich the first year and you won't be disappointed.

Remember, these figures are estimates based on the experiences of desktop publishing services across the nation. Your mileage may vary.

Should you add an employee? Only if you are certain that you will increase income by at least 2.5 times the employee's salary. For example, to hire an employee at $20,000 a year (about $10 an hour), make sure the employee's services will bring you at least $50,000 in business during the coming year. That's a minimum. Some service businesses use multipliers of three or even four to determine whether they can afford to hire additional staff. Remember that about 50 percent of your income will go towards labor costs—that's wages (30 percent of increased sales) and benefits (10 percent of increased sales). As supervisor, you keep the other 10 percent. You'll earn it. Remember that while you work to increase sales you will be reducing your billable time and thus your business's income.

Let's take a closer look at overhead expenses in Figure 1.3. For a typical desktop publishing service you should expect to spend about 40 percent of your income the first year and 30 percent in years after that. Where does it go? Rent will be about 10 percent of sales, office supplies will require another 5 percent, and your telephone about 5 percent. The remaining 20 percent the first year and 5 percent in subsequent years will go for advertising and promotion. The first year's advertising will cost more because you want to get your name out widely and because your advertising won't be as efficient. After

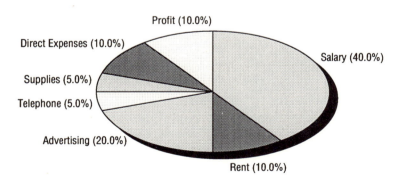

Figure 1.3: Estimated expenses and profits for your first year of operation based on averages of successful desktop publishers.

the first year of advertising, you'll know which media and messages work best for your market.

These estimates are guidelines to help you in calculating income, expenses, and profitability. As your business develops, you may decide to make your salary a higher percentage of sales and reduce the profit or earnings you retain in the business. Or you may find that you can reduce expenses without reducing income by working from your home. Or you may decide to hire a spouse or friend even though it will increase your labor expense. There are many ways you can fine tune your budget. But, to start, stay as close to these percentages as possible. If you spend too little on advertising, for example, your sales may be dramatically reduced.

Do You Really Want to Start a Business?

Certainly, there are many risks involved in starting and running your own business, no matter what type of business it is. But you can minimize these risks by understanding what you're getting into—the purpose of this book—and knowing how to get out of it if you must. Never enter a room without an exit.

A major risk to starting your desktop publishing service is that you will lose your investment of time and money. How can you minimize these risks? Some desktop publishers start their service at home in their spare time, while working another job. This structure presents a number of challenges, but they can be overcome. The business can depend on an answering service or a relative to handle phone inquiries. In fact, a desktop publishing service can turn this limitation to an advantage, offering evening and weekend appointments that competitors do not.

The most successful desktop publishing services are those that operate from a retail shop near their clients. This can also be the most expensive operation, as rent in a successful business district can be high. You may be tempted to locate your new desktop publishing service in a lower-rent area to reduce financial risks. Don't! You'll actually be increasing your financial risks because a poor location will cause a higher percentage of income to be spent on rent. For example, a high-rent store may cost $1,200 a month but bring you $12,000 in business in a month, costing 10 percent of income, while a $600-a-month store may only bring you $3,000 in business each month—20 percent of income. Cheap can actually increase risk.

An alternative to high rent is shared rent. That is, you may be able to sublease a desk or office from another business. This can be especially effective if the landlord is a print shop or related business with which you can share clients. You'll be increasing income while you reduce risk. I'll cover offices in greater detail in Chapter 4.

The best way to minimize risks is to understand what they are and prepare for those from which you cannot recover. You'll want fire insurance. You'll want sufficient operating capital to get you through the first three to six months of your business. You'll want only minimal paper stock. You'll want to come up with alternative services to ensure that you have income. You'll want to make sure that any leases you sign can be renegotiated if your business doesn't work out. Simply, you'll want to make sure you have sufficient exits before you enter.

Action Guidelines

This introduction to starting your own desktop publishing service has given you an overview of the business to help you determine if it is right for you. To help you make that decision, here are some actions you can take today:

✔ Start a desktop publishing notebook, writing down ideas and the answers to Action Guideline questions.

✔ Check your local phone book's Yellow Pages under DESKTOP PUBLISHING or TYPESETTING to see who your competition might be.

✔ Read the Services section of newspapers in your area to determine who is offering desktop publishing services and how they advertise.

✔ Select one or two leading desktop publishing services in your area and hire them to produce a document for you.

✔ Do some rough calculations of your potential income and expenses based on guidelines in this chapter.

✔ Make a list of the risks you would face by starting your own desktop publishing service.

✔ Talk to others about your ideas to get fresh perspectives on them.

Chapter 2

REQUIREMENTS FOR DESKTOP PUBLISHING SERVICES

What will you need to start and operate a successful desktop publishing service? Certainly you will need design skills, some money, and some customers. But just as necessary is a personal desire to help others. This is important if you are an employee; it is vital if you are the owner. As consumers, we can easily read the attitude of people who serve us. We know the difference between people helping us because it's their job or those who truly enjoy doing their job. And we usually respond by supporting and recommending those who help us solve our problems and make us feel important. They appreciate our business—and they get it.

Before you decide whether operating a desktop publishing service is for you, you must know who *you* is. What do you feel most comfortable doing? Under what conditions do you enjoy working with people? Under what conditions do you prefer to avoid people? What are your personal goals? What are your financial goals? How much risk do you feel comfortable taking? Most important, is a desktop publishing service a good fit in your life or will it cause more problems than it cures? Self-analysis can be difficult, but it is the only way of ensuring that this or any other goal will bring you the results you want in your life.

Assessing Your Personal Goals

Maybe by this stage in your life you've developed a list of personal goals for the next year, five years, and beyond. Most people have not. It isn't mandatory that you develop a long list of your life's goals before you start a desktop publishing service or other business, but it will increase your chances of personal and financial success.

A goal is an objective. It is somewhere you want to be or something you want to have. It can be the goal of owning your own desktop publishing service. Or it may be the option of working at home. Or it can be amassing $1 million in assets within 20 years to fund your retirement. Whatever your goals, they are personal and reflect who you are and what you want from your life.

Here are some questions you can answer for yourself to help determine what you enjoy doing and what you want to do about it.

- Is there anything about which people often compliment you? A talent, hobby, or skill?
- Is there some job or task you would do even if you weren't paid?
- Is there some cause or mission that drives you?
- Is there some opportunity that strikes you as worthwhile?

Assessing Your Personal Values

Values are tools that will take you toward your personal goals. Values are standards or qualities that you've established to help you make daily decisions. Those people who succeed in any business have common personal values. Let's look at those values to determine your strengths and opportunities.

Self-Awareness. The process of starting and operating any business is difficult. It will require that you constantly test yourself, standing firm for what works and changing what doesn't. But that's what many people love about being a business owner—the endless challenges. It encourages self-awareness and continual growth.

Hard Work. The great thing about being an *independent* businessperson is that *you* get to select which 12 hours of the day you're going to work! It's true. As you start and grow your desktop publishing you'll spend at least eight hours a day producing your product and another two to six hours marketing and administrating it. Don't expect to work a 40 hour week—at least for awhile—and you won't be disappointed.

Discipline. Discipline is the power behind hard work. You can know exactly what needs to be done and still not do it. Self-discipline forces you to act. Having goals that are meaningful to you will increase your self-discipline.

Independence. Great business owners often make poor employees. They're too independent. They cannot, however, be stubborn. Business owners must maintain a balance between independence and open-mindedness to succeed.

Self-Confidence. It takes a lot of nerve to start a business. It takes a lot more to make it successful. But nerve or self-confidence isn't ego. It's a belief, founded on past successes, in your unique skills. You know you can successfully operate a desktop publishing service because you have the skills, not just the desire to do so.

Adaptability. Life is chaos. No matter how much we plan, people and events change. Products change. Markets change.

We change. A successful business owner must adapt to these changes. Without change, life becomes very dull.

Judgment. To succeed in business, you must make good decisions every day. Wisdom requires knowledge. You must be able to gather complete and accurate facts and make the best decision you can make from those facts. You will not be right every time, but you will be right most of the time. This is good judgment.

Stress Tolerance. Stress is defined as "the confusion created when one's mind overrides the body's basic desire to clobber some yo-yo who desperately deserves it." Humor can help reduce stress. Stress is a part of everyday life, especially in business. Learning to live with stress without taking it personally can help you succeed in business.

Need to Achieve. Success is the achievement of something you go after. It may be the completion of a project, or the start of a business, or the learning of a new skill. This need is a driving force within successful business owners that helps give them the energy to reach their goal.

Assessing Your Financial Goals

As much as you may love producing documents and helping people, you must also have financial goals. Without a fair salary and profit, you won't be able to help people for very long.

What is an appropriate financial goal for your desktop publishing service? One that funds your other goals. If your business goal is to open a new desktop publishing service office each year for three years, your financial goal must be one that will fund such an ambitious goal. If your business goal is to build a successful desktop publishing service then sell it and retire, your financial goal must match the expected selling price of your business. If your business goal is to make a good salary as well as a fair return on your investment, you must first determine what are a good salary and a fair return for you.

One successful desktop publishing service owner established a financial goal of developing annual sales of $100,000 within two years in order to launch a local newspaper. He then wanted to spend five more years building the newspaper before selling controlling interest in it and pursuing other publishing projects. His goals were specific and attainable.

Assessing Your Risk Tolerance

Business is legalized gambling. When you start a business, you're gambling that you will succeed. You're also facing the risk that you will fail and face personal and financial loss. How much does this risk bother you? How much risk can you tolerate?

Everyone's risk tolerance level is different. Some people cannot afford to lose a dime. Of course, as they say in Las Vegas, "One who can't afford to lose can't afford to gamble." Others say, "I started with nothing. Anything I get is a gain." Still others determine potential losses and say, "It's worth the gamble, but I'm going to do whatever I can to improve the odds."

You must determine your own risk tolerance and that of those with whom you share your life. If you're ready to take the plunge, but your spouse would rather not, you need to agree on an acceptable level of risk before starting your business. Otherwise, you may find—as too many people have—that you've traded your invaluable relationship for a replaceable business.

Desktop Publishing Tools

A variety of tools can make your desktop publishing service more efficient and more profitable, including computers, software, printers, copiers, reference books, answering machines, fax machines, desks, chairs, and stationery. Here's an overview of the primary desktop publishing tools available to you. Find a qualified adviser who can help you make the most appropriate selections for your venture and skills.

Computers

A computer is a prerequisite for your desktop publishing service. You'll use a computer to enter text, design documents, add illustrations, and send data files to others. Your computer will also drive your laser printer, another important desktop publishing tool.

People are often apprehensive about computers because of all the new terminology that they must decipher: CPUs, bits, bytes, bauds, networks, boards, hard disks, RAM, monitor interlacing, and on and on. Don't worry about it. You'll quickly pick up what the terms mean. Here's a simplified introduction to computers—or, for you, it may be a review. I'll cover IBM-compatible computers as well as Apple Macintosh computers. Macs use a different operating system, but the basics are the same. Both are widely used for desktop publishing (Figure 2.1).

CPUs. A *CPU* is a central processing unit. It is an electronic machine built around a small microprocessor, also called a chip, that processes information for you.

The CPU is typically called by the same name as the microprocessor chip that is its brain. As an example, early personal computers (PCs) used a microprocessor chip called the 8088 (eighty eighty-eight). So they were called 88s or by the IBM brand name for the model, the XT. The next generation microprocessor and CPU was the 80286, referred to as the 286 (two eighty-six) or by the IBM brand model, the AT. Then came the 386, the 486, and the 586, or Intel Pentium microprocessor and CPU. Apple Macintoshes use Motorola

68030, 68040, and Power PC chips. Macs are purchased as a complete computer so you don't get the option—or frustration—of selecting between various chip configurations. Popular Mac models include the Quadra series and the new Power PC.

The next number to remember in looking at CPUs is the *clock speed*. XT chips had a clock speed of about 5 MHz (mega—or million—hertz). Today's 486 and newer microprocessors have clock speeds of 50 MHz and more! Some use internal technology to double the clock speed, such as the 486DX2/66, which doubles the speed of a 33 MHz chip to run at 66 MHz.

So all you really need to know about buying a PC is that a 486 is faster than a 286 or 386, and a clock speed of 66 MHz is faster than one that's 33 MHz. However, if your work involves color graphics, clock speed can make a difference.

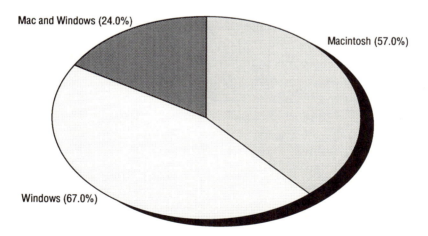

Figure 2.1: Desktop publishers use Apple Macintosh and IBM-compatible PCs with Microsoft Windows or both to perform their services. Source: *NADTP Journal* study.

Fortunately, there's not more than a few hundred dollars difference between fast and super-fast.

Data travels through a computer on a highway called a *bus*. How that highway is set up and managed is called the bus architecture. Rather than get side-tracked with a technical explanation on the advantages and disadvantages of system busses, select a computer with an EISA (Extended Industry Standard Architecture) bus for your desktop publishing system.

RAM. A computer uses a work area where data is gathered and processed. This place is called the *random access memory* or *RAM.* The amount of RAM is measured in *bytes* or computer (not English) words it can hold, the units used are Megabytes (Mb; 1,000 bytes). Depending on the size of the programs and graphics you will be using, your PC's RAM should be at least 8Mb with the option of later upgrading to at least 64 Mb later. Older PCs offered between 0.5 and 1Mb of RAM, but today's PC typically come with 4 to 32Mb. The larger this work area is, the more work that can be done simultaneously.

Hard Disks. The *hard disk* drives in your PC can hold thousands of pages of information on stacked disks that look like miniature LP records stacked on a record player. The hard disk knows where to look for any information stored on it and it can access the information in a small fraction of a second.

Hard disk storage, like RAM, is measured in megabytes (Mb). Older PCs were equipped with hard disk of 10Mb, 20Mb, or 40Mb. Newer PCs store 120Mb, 240Mb, 360Mb, or even a gigabyte (Gb; 1 billion bytes) or more. To put that in terms that are more real, a 1Gb hard disk can theoretically store about a half-million typed pages. Larger hard drives are necessary for desktop publishing because each graphic image is 1Mb or more in size.

Your hard drive interfaces to the computer using one of two technologies: IDE (integrated drive electronics) or SCSI (small computer systems interface). SCSI, pronounced scuzzy, is better for graphics.

Diskette Drives. Data can be moved from one PC to another using small, portable diskettes. These diskettes, sometimes called *floppies*, can store from a third of a megabyte to up to nearly three megabytes of information. Then, once you've written your desktop document or drawn your plans, you can remove the data by instructing the PC to copy it to a diskette.

Another option are the removable drives. A couple of choices in this area are SyQuest or Bernoulli. They attach to your computer and allow you to place up to 44 or 88Mb of information onto a disk. The disk may then be removed for output from a service bureau or used as a backup to your entire system. This is also an excellent method of storing older files that may be used again, rather than keeping them on your hard drive. These drives are especially useful for color graphic work as the files tend to be large.

Diskette Format and Density. In the past ten years since PCs have become popular, a number of diskettes of different formats and densities have evolved. When the computer's operating system formats a disk, it gives directions on how information is stored on its surface. Diskettes come in different sizes and densities. Density refers to the surface of magnetic particles on the disk and determines how much information can be spread. Earlier diskettes were 5¼ inches square, and were made of a thin, round plastic disk placed in a bendable (hence the name "floppy") plastic sleeve and sealed. As technology developed, the storage capacity of disks increased. The first diskettes held 360 Kb (kilobytes; 1,000 bytes), and quickly multiplied to 1,200 Kb or 1.2 Mb. Many PCs still use this format.

Another format soon emerged, the 3½-inch diskette with a thin, round plastic diskette housed in a hard plastic case. The first popular format stored 720K or twice that of the larger 5¼ diskette of the time. Double-density, 3½-inch diskettes hold

100K, and high-density, 1.44Mb. The newest format can store up to 2.88Mb of information on a diskette that will fit into a shirt pocket!

Monitor. Your computer will also require a *monitor*, similar to a TV screen where your document is displayed. A monochrome (black and white) monitor is least expensive but not practical for desktop publishing unless you're certain you won't be using color in your business. Color monitors are easier to read—and more attractive—but also more expensive. SVGA (super video graphics array) monitors are today's cost-effective standard. The screen should be 15 to 21 inches in size with the price going up proportionally. Resolution is measured in dots, called a dot pitch. As you will be on your computer many hours a day, get a monitor with a 0.28 mm or lower dot pitch. Also make sure your video card matches your monitor selection. Your computer retailer or consultant can help you select the appropriate monitor and video board. The monitor is an important piece of equipment for the desktop publishing business and is worth researching.

Scanner. How can you get printed images into your desktop publishing system? With a scanner. A scanner looks like a fax machine without the phone and keyboard. You feed in a sheet (or pass a hand-held scanner over the image) and it is transferred as a graphics file to your computer.

Scanners are expensive for someone who doesn't use them daily. A basic black-and-white scanner will cost $500 while a high-resolution (9,600 dpi) color scanner will cost $3,000 or more. An alternative is to find a service bureau who can scan your images into your preferred format. The $5 or $10 charge is much less expensive than having a scanner that you rarely use.

A second use for your scanner is in conjunction with a computer fax board to serve as your fax machine. By doing so, you're saving the cost of a $300 to $600 fax.

One final hardware element you will need is "electronic insurance"—line and power protection hardware to protect yourself from electrical blackout, brownout, or power surge that could wipe out an hour's or a week's work. A UPS (uninterruptable power supply) with line conditioning can be purchased for $100 to $500—cheap electrical insurance.

Apple Macintosh. Selecting an Apple Macintosh computer makes building a desktop publishing system somewhat easier, but also reduces the options. Macs are intended to be more user friendly than the IBM and compatibles. They are. In fact, only with the advent of Windows 3.0 did DOS PCs approach the Mac in ease of use. Desktop publishing actually started on Macs and has since moved to the DOS and Windows operating systems. Two of the most popular desktop publishing software programs, Aldus PageMaker and Quark XPress, were first developed for Macs.

The reason why the Mac is considered more user friendly is because of its graphical user interface; that is, the use of icons or small images to represent complex commands. While Microsoft Windows also offers this feature, the Mac has a foothold in desktop publishing and many prefer it. Macs are easier to set up because fewer options are offered. You don't need to know about ROM BIOS. You select your unit from a handful of models, load software from a smaller selection of well-designed programs, and you're in business. Fewer options is both good and bad.

But what if you have need for both an IBM-compatible PC and a Mac? There are numerous software and hardware products that will help you link the two systems and exchange files. So your client can furnish text produced on a PC using WordPerfect and you can design their newsletter on the Mac using PageMaker. Utilities such as SoftPC (Insignia Solutions, 526 Clyde Ave., Mountain View CA 94043; 800-848-7677) allow DOS applications to run on a Macintosh. The Apple

Power Macintosh uses the Motorola Power PC microprocessor that can run Macintosh, OS/2, MS-DOS, Windows, Windows NT, and UNIX software.

There is a pricing premium to buying Apple Macintosh hardware: about 20 to 30 percent. However, software is about the same cost whether you select the DOS or Mac version, with a few exceptions.

Computer Software

With an understanding of the basics of computers, you can better see how computer programs can work for you. And, even though computer hardware is discussed here first, you will probably select the computer programs or software before you choose the computer or hardware to run it on.

A computer program is a set of instructions written in a language that your computer understands. The program can be as simple as a word processor or as complex as a database publisher. Let's look at the function of each category of computer software.

Operating Systems. DOS stands for disk operating system that comes with your computer and translates commands like copy into a language that your PC understands. The most widely used DOS is MS-DOS developed by Microsoft Corp. IBM has its own version, called PC DOS. Novell DOS was developed by Digital Research, now owned by Novell. OS/2 is another popular operating system, though there aren't currently many desktop publishing programs written for it. Macintosh computers use Apple System operating system.

Shell programs make your PC easier to use and perform a number of important maintenance functions. It's called a shell because it wraps around the less-friendly DOS program to make it easier to copy, delete, and manage files. Some shell programs also include "utilities" or special programs that help you keep your data organized and safe.

Windows is a shell program, developed by Microsoft that lets you open a number of overlapping boxes or windows on your computer screen, each with different programs in them. You can be writing a letter and when a client calls quickly switch to a window with information about the client and your current project. If you expect to network or tie computers together electronically for sharing files, consider Windows for Workgroups.

Some of the following software programs mentioned in the following sections are available only for IBM-compatible PCs, others are just for Apple Macintoshes, and a growing number can be purchased for either. Check with your computer supplier for availability and recommendations.

Word Processors. Word processors simply process words. That is, they let you type words into the computer, move them around, insert words, take some out, and make any changes you want before you print them on paper. You can use word processors to produce documents for clients or to write letters to suppliers and prospects. I've used computer word processors for more than ten years and would never go back to manual or even electric typewriters. Word processors let you change your mind.

In addition, many popular word processing programs allow you to perform many of the tasks of desktop publishing systems: select typefaces, format text, and import graphics. They are considered document processors rather than just word processors. In fact, many successful desktop publishing services use these word processors for all text and production.

Common word processing programs include WordPerfect, Microsoft Word, Ami Pro, WordStar, and XyWrite. Each has its own unique features and following. Some are more user friendly than others. WordPerfect is one of the most widely used word processors, especially among desktop publishers.

Ami Pro is probably the friendliest. Microsoft Word is popular for users of Microsoft Windows. Major Macintosh programs are Microsoft Word, MacWrite, and WordPerfect.

Desktop Publishers. There is a wide variety of desktop publishing software offered to fit varied needs, budgets, and systems. Simply, desktop publishing software transforms text and art into finished documents that can be taken to a commercial printer for reproduction. For short quantities, the documents can be printed using a laser printer. A desktop publishing system imports text from a word processor, changes it to a specified typeface, allows you to add illustrations and other graphic elements, and prepares it for the printer.

The most popular desktop publishing systems include Aldus PageMaker, Quark XPress, Corel Ventura, Microsoft Publisher, and Frame Technology FrameMaker (Figure 2.2). Macintosh programs are PageMaker, Quark XPress, ReadySetGo, and Ventura Publisher. Most of these applications can use *templates,* or format guides, to simplify the devel-

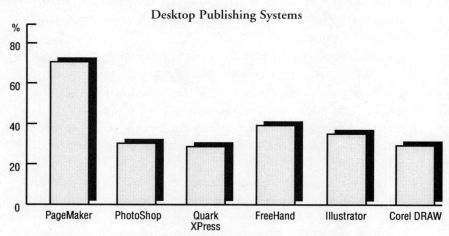

Figure 2.2: Desktop publishers use a variety of computer programs. (Source: *NADTP Journal* study.)

opment of specific documents. You can purchase templates for producing business cards, mailing labels, brochures, envelopes, and other documents.

Type Fonts. A type font is type design that uses a similar look for all letters in the alphabet. Typewriters use a type face called Courier. Many newspapers use Times Roman or a similar type face. Headlines in newspapers and books often use a variation of the Helvetica type face. Producers of type faces include Adobe PostScript, Agfa, Bitstream, and Monotype. There are a variety of firms packaging common type fonts. Make sure they match your printer's capabilities.

Art. Desktop publishing incorporates not only words but also illustrations, called graphics, which include photos, line drawings, charts, forms, and other nontype elements. Which art production programs you use depends on what you do. If you primarily develop newsletters for clients, you will use a photo production package and a drawing package. In addition, you will purchase packages of predrawn art, called clip art. If you publish intricate engineering drawings you will use computer-aid design or CAD programs.

Popular art programs include CorelDRAW, PhotoStyler, Harvard Graphics, Visio, AutoSketch, AutoCAD, Adobe Illustrator, Aldus Freehand, Lotus Freelance Graphics, MacDraw Pro, Micrografx Designer, Adobe Photoshop, Micrografx Picture Publisher, and ClickArt. Mac programs include SuperPaint, Canvas, DeskPaint, and MacDraw. There are many, many others.

Optical Character Recognition. Retyping a long document into your word processor can be tedious and inaccurate. Fortunately, there are electronic tools that can help you. The tools are called optical character recognizers, or OCRs. Used with a scanner, these software programs read the characters on the page and translate them into alphabetic letters. Some even check words against an electronic dictionary to improve accuracy. You can even set them up to read incoming faxes and convert them to an editable text file.

There are many OCRs available with price tags from $80 to $500 and more. They include Caere OmniPage Professional, Calera WordScan, Expervision TypeReader, Optical Mark Reading Software, Recognita OCR, and Xerox TextBridge. Mac programs are AccuText, OmniPage, Oldvai Read It, or TypeReader.

Spreadsheets. A spreadsheet arranges and calculates numbers into a meaningful form for accuracy. It's named after the wide multicolumnar sheets that accountants use to make journal entries. You will soon find many uses for a spreadsheet software program.

As an example, for about a hundred dollars you can purchase a basic spreadsheet program that will let you enter horizontal rows or lines of job expense names (Income, Expenses, etc.) and vertical columns of numbers. Most important, you can instruct the program to make calculations on rows, columns and cells and it will do so in less than a second. If you update a number, it automatically recalculates the spreadsheet for you.

Fancier and more costly spreadsheets can follow your written instructions, called macros, to do special calculations automatically. You may want to write a macro that will select all of the invoices over 60 days past due and total them up. Better spreadsheets will also produce graphs and pie charts that impress lenders and other financial types.

Popular spreadsheet programs for PCs include Lotus 1-2-3, Borland Quattro Pro, and Microsoft Excel. Mac programs include Excel, Microsoft Works, Lotus 1-2-3, and Wingz.

Databases. A database software program is much like an index card file box. You can record and store thousands or even millions of pieces of information. But a database program is even better than a file box because it finds information in the files in a fraction of a second.

The most common application of a database program for desktop publishing services is a client file. If you only have a few clients, this may not be necessary. But as you add clients, prospects, and other business contacts you may soon need at least a simple database program to keep track of them.

Your prospect/client database will contain such information as name, address, city and state, zip code, phone and fax numbers, contact names, annual budget information, list of projects you've completed for them, information about their business, even their hobbies. Then, if you want to find out how many of your clients are located in a specific city and haven't purchased any services from you within the last year, you simply tell your database program to search its files for you. It's that easy.

Popular database programs for PCs include Borland Paradox, Microsoft Access, Lotus Approach, and Microsoft FoxPro. Macintosh programs are FileMaker, 4th Dimension, and others. Depending on which word processor and spreadsheet you select, you may want to purchase a database program produced by the same company. That is, if you use Lotus' Ami Pro and 1-2-3, choose their database program, Approach. The operating logic of each software developer differs slightly but is similar within its own product line.

Integrated Programs. You can also find integrated software programs that combine the three primary programs: word processor, spreadsheet, and database. Ask your local computer store to recommend a good integrated program. Some also include other related programs such as communications software that lets your PC talk to other PCs over the phone using modems. The cost of a good quality integrated system is usually much less than the total price for the individual components.

The communication feature in some integrated programs is a nice plus. Your word processor could include financial figures from your spreadsheet in your correspondence, then send the document by modem to someone listed in your database. Just as important, an integrated group of programs developed by a single software firm will have similar commands in each program. You won't have to learn three separate programs, you'll learn one larger program.

Integrated programs are especially recommended for those who don't want to spend a lot of time selecting and learning numerous software programs. Popular integrated programs include Microsoft Works, ClarisWorks, Lotus SmartSuite, Borland Office, and Microsoft Office.

CD-ROM Drives

Digital recording and storage has dramatically advanced the reliability and availability of music and information. The same technology that gives us CDs or compact disks also offers data storage using CD-ROM. ROM stands for read-only memory, meaning the information is placed on the disk once and can be read many times. Data on the disk cannot be changed easily.

CD-ROM drives were an expensive toy just a couple of years ago, costing $1,000 or more—and there were few disks available. Today you can add a CD-ROM drive added to your computer for less than $300 and access a broad world of information. Each disk holds about 680 Mb of information. About a third of all desktop publishers use CD-ROM (Figure 2.3).

CD-ROM is especially popular with desktop publishers as it offers a method of selecting from thousands of typefaces, graphics images, data, and other resources quickly and easily. In fact, many desktop publishing systems are offering their product on CD-ROM to reduce hard drive requirements and make updates easier to install.

In purchasing a CD-ROM drive, look for a SCSI interface with access time under 200 ms (yep, microseconds), and

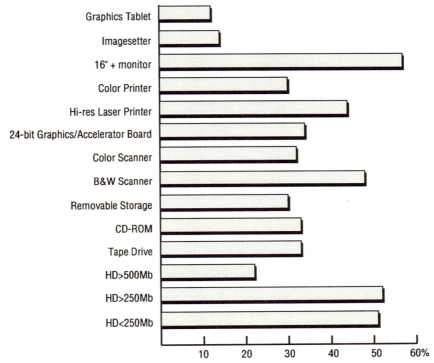

Figure 2.3: CD-ROM is one of many computer peripherals used by successful desktop publishing services. (Source: *NADTP Journal* study).

either double- or triple-speed seek. A double-speed seek can transfer data at 300 Kb a second or faster.

More expensive—for now—are erasable optical CD systems. Desktop publishers are using them to publish directly to CD rather than to paper. Catalogs and other large documents, for example, can be published to CD disks and quickly mailed to subscribers or customers faster than they can be commercially printed. CD-ROM recorders are currently priced between $3,500 and $7,000 each, but as with most technology will come down in price over the next few years.

Printers

Desktop documents must be sent from your computer to a printer to be printed on paper. There are many types of printers to select from. But we only need to cover the basics of them here so you'll know which ones to look for as you go shopping.

Dot Matrix. The dot matrix printer forms letters from a bunch of dots. A nine-pin printer uses nine tiny pins—three rows of three—to form each letter. The 24-pin printer does the same job but uses 24 pins—four rows of six. So the letters formed by a 24-pin printer are easier to read than that of a nine-pin printer. Today, most dot matrix printers use 24 pins. Dot matrix printers are acceptable for drafts, but cannot be used for quality reproduction.

Laser. A laser is simply a beam of light that's focused by a mirror. A small laser in your printer actually writes the characters by magnetizing a piece of paper, black dust called toner is passed over it and sticks to the places the laser light touched, then the sheet travels through a heater that fuses the black toner to the paper. A light-emitting-diode (or LED) printer works in virtually the same way.

Bubble Jet. Similar to the laser, the bubble jet printer sprays special ink on to the page in patterns cut by heat. Bubble jet printers are typically less expensive than laser printers.

Laser/LED and ink jet printers are available that can print highly accurate color documents using solid ink, thermal wax, color jet, and other processes. Color printers are more expensive, but they are necessary for some types of desktop publishing.

When shopping for a laser printer, make sure the resolution, measured in dots-per-inch (dpi), is sufficient for your work. For business correspondence, 300 dpi is sufficient. For reproduction in newspapers and for proofs, 600 dpi is best. For brochures, newsletters, and magazines, 1,200 dpi or 2,400 dpi is usually required. If you only need 1,200+ dpi once in awhile, you can save money by purchasing a 600 or lower dpi printer and sending your final electronic files to a service bureau (advertised in desktop publishing magazines) for final printing. The same goes for color printing—use a service bureau if you only do color printing occasionally.

Here's another term you'll need to know—PostScript. You'll hear it in reference to printers, but it is actually a page description language. It tells the computer printer how to form characters and graphics for printing. It is developed and licensed by Adobe Systems. PostScript is a standard between software, typefaces, and printers that makes desktop publishing easier, though slightly more expensive.

Copiers

Copy machines can be very useful to your desktop publishing. You will want to conveniently copy brochures, correspondence, plans, proposals, contracts, agreements, procedures, and other business documents. A good copier can be purchased for under $800. If you're producing a client newsletter, your own brochures, direct mail pieces, or other marketing documents, your copy machine can be more cost-effective than running down to the copy shop or printer for a few copies every day.

Features you will want to look for in a copier may include enlargement and reduction, paper trays, collating of multiple copies, and reproduction of photos. Depending on what document packages you sell, you may want a copier that can produce duplex copies, or print on both sides of the sheet. Or you may want a copier that prints on 11 x 17 sheets for professional four-page documents. Determine your copying needs before you buy.

The most popular copier brands are Canon, Sharp, Mita, Toshiba, and Minolta.

Fax Machines

There are more than 25 million fax machines in the world, with most of them installed in businesses. The concept of the fax machine is simple: it "reads" a sheet of paper for light and dark spots much like a copy machine does. It then converts these spots into a code that's sent across a telephone line at a speed of nearly 10,000 bits of information per second. Based on some international standards, the fax machine on the other end knows how to read these signals and convert them into light and dark spots that conform to the image that was sent. This image is printed on a piece of paper and you have a facsimile, or fax.

The desktop publisher can now send documents, letters, proposals, sales literature, copies of invoices, and other printed material to prospects, clients, and others in just seconds. A typical one-page fax takes less than a minute to transmit on a Group-3 fax machine. It, too, is dramatically changing the way that businesses conduct business.

Facsimile machines look like small printers with a tray to hold outgoing paper and a telephone set either attached or nearby. You call the fax number and your fax machine sends out a tone that tells the other fax machine it would like to transmit a facsimile. The receiving machine sends your machine a high-pitched tone and you manually press your machine's start button and hang up the phone. The fax is being transmitted. Some machines automate the process and you simply put the copy into the machine and press a button that calls a specific telephone in memory and sends the fax without any help.

There are dozens of features to consider when buying a fax machine for your business. However, many are frills. Most important is that your fax machine is Group-3 compatible.

Beyond that, explain to the salesperson what you need your fax machine for and let him or her show you the newest features and whistles. You can get a basic fax machine for $300-$400, a better one for $400-$800, and your heart's desire for a thousand dollars or more. Or you can rent or lease a fax machine. The more expensive fax machines will print on plain paper rather than slick thermal paper that has a tendency to curl.

Some fax machines will combine other functions, such as a standard telephone handset that you can use for your primary or secondary business line. Some also include a tape or digital answering machine. This setup is practical because you have the business phone line feeding into one machine that can serve three purposes: let you answer, take messages, or take faxes. But, like any machine that combines functions, if one goes out or becomes obsolete, they may all go. Compare the cost of a combined unit against the cost of individual units. If there is little difference, go for the separate components.

Also consider PC fax boards. They are printed circuit boards that are installed inside your computer and allow you to plug it into a phone and use it as a fax. There are even models that will serve as your answering machine as well. Fax boards are typically purchased through computer stores.

Computer software can let you fax desktop documents, letters, and other documents directly from your computer without printing them first to paper. Leading fax programs include Caere Fax and Find, BIT Software BitFax Professional, Delrina WinFax Pro, and Phoenix Eclipse FAX OCR.

Other Publishing Equipment

There are many other valuable pieces of equipment a desktop publishing service can have, depending on what products and services they offer. Desktop publishers may have digital cameras, binders, platemakers, collators, sorters, folders, trimmers, drill punches, and stitchers.

Desktop Publishing Supplies

The paper you select is an important part of your product. Professional desktop publishing services stock a wide selection of papers and forms to match the needs of clients. Standard paper as you would buy in most stores is called bond. Paper with parallel fibers that give a ribbed-effect is called laid paper. Paper with cloth content is called linen. Basis weight is the weight of the paper, in pounds, of a ream of a specific size. Most bond paper is 16-lb., 20-lb., or 22-lb. paper.

How much paper should you stock? That depends. If you have a nearby source for paper that will let you purchase in small quantities while earning a discount, you only need to stock what you will use within a few days. However, if your source must ship preferred stock to you, always keep on hand at least a week's stock and preferably two week's stock.

One successful desktop publisher keeps at least a month's stock on hand at all times. She makes a physical inventory at the end of each month and orders replacement stock at that time. This procedure minimizes the time dedicated to inventory control while keeping down the amount of cash she has tied up in paper inventory. She estimates her average paper inventory to be worth between $800 and $1,200.

Chapter 3 will include information on resources for desktop document papers.

Calculating Your Business' Financial Requirements

How much money will you need to build a profitable desktop publishing service? Figure 2.4 will help you make a preliminary estimate of your business' financial requirements. These estimates will be revised and expanded in future chapters.

Financial Worksheet

Estimated Start-Up Costs
Office preparation $ _____
Office equipment $ _____
Initial office supplies $ _____
Initial paper inventory $ _____
Telephone, answering machine $ _____
Utility deposits $ _____
Licenses and permits $ _____
Insurance $ _____
Professionals $ _____
Signs $ _____
Initial advertising $ _____
Miscellaneous expenses $ _____
Total Estimated Start-Up Costs $ _____

Estimated Operating Costs
Living expenses $ _____
Employee salaries $ _____
Rent $ _____
Utilities $ _____
Advertising $ _____
Insurance $ _____
Office supplies $ _____
Replacement paper inventory $ _____
Taxes $ _____
Equipment maintenance $ _____
Total Estimated Operating Costs $ _____

Estimated Financial Resources
Assets
    Checking and savings $ _____
    CDs and securities $ _____
    Owed to you $ _____
    Real estate $ _____
    Autos and vehicles $ _____
    Insurance cash value $ _____
    Other assets $ _____
    Total assets $ _____
Liabilities
    Credit cards $ _____
    Household credit $ _____
    Auto loans $ _____
    Taxes $ _____
    Education loans $ _____
    Mortgages $ _____
    Other liabilities $ _____
    Total liabilities $ _____
Total Net Worth $ _____

Figure 2.4: This financial worksheet can help you estimate start-up and operating costs as well as financial resources for your desktop publishing service.

To estimate start-up costs, you will need to make your best guess of how much it will cost to set up your office for the day you open the door to your first customer. These costs include preparing and equipping your office, getting required licenses and professional memberships, getting the phone hooked up, and funding your initial advertising.

Estimating operating costs can be more difficult because it requires that you estimate your living expenses. Most people who have been employees spend as much as they make; they're not sure exactly what they *need* to live on. However, by starting with your current net (after taxes) salary, you can roughly calculate whether you require more or less to live on. If you operate your business as a sole proprietor (discussed further in Chapter 4), your personal income taxes and self-employment (social security) tax will be paid by the business, which is synonymous with yourself.

Other operating costs are those expenses that you will pay each month to keep the doors open (fixed or overhead expenses) as well as those that increase as sales increase (variable expenses).

Where can you get the money you need to start your business? Earnings from job, savings, credit cards, cash settlements, inheritances, retirement funds, credit union loans, life insurance policy equity, home equity line of credit, personal loans, supplier loans or credit, SBA Microloans. You'll learn how to use your financial resources—and develop new ones—in Chapter 7.

Action Guidelines

You've learned the requirements of starting and operating a successful desktop publishing service. They include evaluating your personal and financial goals as well as your tolerance for risk, reviewing the tools you need, and calculating financial requirements. Here's how to implement what you've learned in this chapter.

✔ Using your desktop publishing business notebook, make notes regarding your personal goals and values, your financial goals, and your tolerance for risk. Be as honest as possible.

✔ Begin looking at computers, printers, and software for your desktop publishing service. Don't buy yet; just start learning what you can about them.

✔ Complete the financial worksheet in this chapter to determine how much you'll need and where you can get it.

✔ List the skills you'll need to enhance or acquire to make your desktop publishing service successful. How can you develop or improve on these skills?

✔ Review your desktop publishing service requirements and start thinking about resources, the topic of the next chapter.

Chapter 3

DESKTOP PUBLISHING SERVICE RESOURCES

Desktop publishing cannot be accomplished without extensive resources. A resource is a person, product, or service that can help you with your objectives. Resources for your desktop publishing service include your own experiences, your prospective customers, trade associations, conventions, seminars, training courses, books, magazines, and governmental offices. Together they can increase your working knowledge of desktop documents and of business as well as help you understand how to work efficiently and profitably.

This chapter offers information on these and other resources. Included are addresses and telephone numbers to help you get your desktop publishing service off the ground.

Analyzing Your Own Experiences with Printed Documents

The first and most important resource for your desktop publishing service is you. Your experiences with printed documents may be limited to receiving and reading them. Or you may have experience in designing or printing brochures,

> Take time to review your own experiences with documents.
>
> - With what types of documents are you most familiar?
> - Were there any specific documents or designs that seemed to be most effective?
> - Have you produced documents for others? What types? What publishing tools did you use?
> - How have you used documents in the past?
> - How do you feel documents can be improved?
> - List five or six elements that, in your experience, must be included in an effective document.
>
> In any business, success requires empathy and empathy requires experience. The more you understand about your customer, the better you will be able to serve him or her.

newsletters, and other documents. Or maybe you don't have extensive experience with publishing, but you do have computer skills.

The point is that to serve your customers well you must understand their needs. You must know how they feel, what they need, how they buy, and how they use these documents to increase customer awareness and sales.

Determining Customers' Needs

The best way to understand your customers is to interview them. Find out what they are thinking. Understand what they want from a document and from you. Ask them what is most important to them. Learn what makes them select one desktop publishing service over another.

How can you interview customers before you start your desktop publishing service? By interviewing prospective customers. Talk with friends who own businesses or are decision-makers in a business. Interview the marketing communications managers at major employers in your area. Set up a part-time desktop publishing service, such as on weekends, and interview people who respond to your ad.

In general, you'll learn that your customers want an effective document that clearly presents information in a creative and memorable way. Depending on your chosen clientele, the next most important requirement may be price, speed, or quality. They may need to have a newsletter produced for less than $50 a page, or within 48 hours, or one that will impress an important client. You may learn that two of these three elements—price, speed, quality—are already served in your area and that there is a sufficiently large market for desktop documents that are developed for the third element.

Chapter 6 will cover marketing in greater detail. For now, work toward an understanding of your potential customers' needs.

Trade Associations for Desktop Publishers

A trade association is a group of businesses that agree to share information among themselves regarding their trade. Plumbers have them, car makers have them; so do desktop publishers.

The leading trading association for this profession is the National Association of Desktop Publishers (462 Old Boston St., Topsfield MA 01983; 800-874-4113). The NADTP claims a membership of 13,000. Individual dues are about $100 a year and includes a subscription to the *NADTP Journal* and other benefits.

Another leader is the Association for the Development of Electronic Publishing Technique (360 N. Michigan Ave.,

Suite 1111, Chicago IL 60601; 312-609-0577). The National Association of Secretarial Services (3637 4th St. N., Suite 330, St. Petersburg FL 33704; 800-237-1462) helps desktop publishers as well as secretarial services and business support providers. NASS offers a newsletter, business reports, and toll-free consulting services.

There are many other trade associations for desktop publishing, typesetting, and printing service businesses. They include American Institute of Graphic Arts (1059 Third Ave., New York NY 10021; 212-752-0813), National Composition and Prepress Association (100 Daingerfield Rd., Alexandria VA 22314; 703-519-8122), Typographers International Association (84 Park Ave., Flemington NJ 08822; 908-782-4635) and Printing Industries of America (100 Daingerfield Rd., Alexandria VA 22314; 703-519-8122).

Conventions and Seminars for Desktop Publishers

The Professional Association of Desktop Publishers, Inc. sponsors an annual convention of members. Workshops, guest speakers, and roundtables are organized to encourage desktop publishers from across the country to share information, techniques, and ideas. In addition, there are numerous printing industry association conventions and seminars, including Computer Graphics (301-587-4545) and Graph Expo (703-264-7208).

Valuable Training Courses for Desktop Publishers

CareerTrack (3085 Center Green Drive, Boulder CO 80308; 800-334-1018) offers numerous video and audio training courses for computer programs used by desktop publishers. Topics include Getting Acquainted With Your Computer, WordPerfect, MS-DOS, Microsoft Windows, Microsoft Word, Photoshop, Clarisworks, and PageMaker.

Books for Desktop Publishers

There is a wide variety of books available to help desktop publishers ply their trade. Most are available through local bookstores or by mail from the NADTP Bookstore (462 Old Boston St., Topsfield MA 01983) and other trade sources. Books include:

- *The Illustrated Handbook of Desktop Publishing and Typesetting,* by Michael Kleper (Windcrest Books)
- *Looking Good in Print,* by Roger C. Parker (Ventana Press)
- *Newsletters From the Desktop,* by Roger C. Parker (Ventana Press)
- *The Gray Book,* by Gosney, Odam and Schmal (Ventana Press)
- *The Desktop Publisher's Idea Book,* by Chuck Green (Bantam-ITC)
- *Desktop Publishing Success,* by Felix Kramer and Maggie Lovass (Irwin)
- *The Electronic Type Catalog,* by Steve Byers (Bantam-ITC)
- *Desktop Publishing in Color,* by Michael Kieran (Bantam-ITC)
- *Electronic Design & Publishing Business Practices,* by Liane Sebastian (Allsworth Press)
- *Pricing Guide to Desktop Publishing Services,* by Robert Brenner (Brenner Information Group)
- *Chicago Guide to Preparing Electronic Manuscripts,* (University of Chicago Press)
- *Editing Books and Long Documents on a Computer,* by George Alexander (National Composition and Prepress Association.)

- *Marketing Phototypesetting,* by Ken Chaletzky and Wade Dowdle (National Composition and Prepress Association.)
- *Practical Typography From A to Z,* by Frank Romano (National Composition and Prepress Association.)
- *Publishing with CD-ROM,* by Patti Myers (National Composition and Prepress Association.)

In addition, standard reference books that should be in your office, available at most bookstores, include:

- *The American Heritage Dictionary* (or your favorite)
- *Roget's Thesaurus* or *The Synonym Finder*
- *The Elements of Style, MLA Style Manual,* or *Chicago Manual of Style.*

Magazines and Trade Journals for Desktop Publishers

There are numerous magazines and trade journals for those who publish from the desktop. They include *Publish* (501 Second St., San Francisco CA 94107; 800-685-3435), *Technique* (10 Post Office Square, Suite 600S, Boston MA 02109; 800-272-7377), *NCPA Journal* (100 Daingerfield Rd., Alexandria VA 22314; 703-519-8122), *PRINT* (3200 Tower Oaks Blvd., Rockville MD 20852; 800-222-2654), *Seybold Report on Desktop Publishing* (Box 644, Media PA 19063; 215-565-2480), and, especially for the Macintosh, *The Page* (Box 14493, Chicago IL 60614; 312-348-1200).

Another information resource for desktop publishers is the Desktop Publishing Forum (GO DTPFORUM) CompuServe Information Service (800-848-8990). If you have a modem on your computer and some communications software, you can call up CompuServe and join the forum to talk with other desktop publishers. There are libraries, conferences, and conversations to help you exchange information and ideas amongst colleagues. In addition, you can ask questions of major desktop hardware and software vendors and users. Other on-line services have similar forums.

Considering a Franchise

Franchising is a form of licensing by which the owner (the franchisor) of a product or service distributes through affiliated dealers (the franchisees). The franchise license is typically for a specific geographical area. The product or service is marketed by a brand name (McDonalds, PIP Printing, etc.), and the franchisor controls the way that it is marketed. The franchisor requires consistency among the franchisees: standardized products or services, trademarks, uniform symbols, equipment, and storefronts. The franchisor typically offers assistance in organizing, training, merchandising, and management. In exchange, the franchisor receives initial franchise fees and an ongoing fee based on sales levels.

One useful source of information on available franchises is the *Franchise Opportunities Handbook,* produced and published by the United States Department of Commerce and available through the Superintendent of Documents (U.S. Government Printing Office, Washington DC 20402) or your regional federal bookstore. This handbook lists basic information on franchises available in 44 categories, including the name and address of the franchisor, a description of the operation, number of franchises, how long the franchise has been in business, how much equity capital is needed, how much financial assistance is available, what training is provided, and what managerial assistance is available.

Another source of information on franchises is the International Franchise Association (1350 New York Avenue N.W., Suite 900, Washington DC 20005). The IFA's

Franchise Opportunities Guide is a comprehensive listing of franchisors by industry and business category. *Franchising Opportunities* is their bimonthly magazine. Their newsletter, *Franchising World*, includes information on developing trends in franchising.

Other sources include *Entrepreneur, Income Opportunities,* and other magazines available on most newsstands.

In addition to franchises are business opportunities and resource suppliers. A business opportunity allows you to sell a particular product or service without the strict requirements of a franchise. Depending on the opportunity, you may be licensed to use the name in your advertisement. A supplier will furnish you with a product that you can then resell to your customers.

Sources for Desktop Publishing Papers

Where should you buy desktop document papers and supplies? Local stationery stores may be able to furnish any papers you need at discount prices. They can also advise you on paper selection.

As the business of desktop publishing is growing so is the availability of quality papers. Paper Direct (205 Chubb Ave., Lyndhurst NJ 07071; 800-272-7377), BeaverPrints (305 Main St., Bellwood PA 16617; 800-923-2837), Paper Design Warehouse (1720 Oak St., Lakewood NJ 08701; 800-836-5400), Premier Papers (P.O. Box 64785, St. Paul MN 55164; 800-843-0414) and Idea Art (P.O. Box 291505, Nashville TN 37229; 800-433-2278) have revolutionized the business with well-designed papers and forms that can be run through a laser printer for high-quality results. They offer preprinted sheets for letterheads, envelopes, brochures, certificates, labels, folders, business cards, note cards, and other documents.

Some of these suppliers sell sample kits that you can refer to as you design projects. The kits typically include tri-fold or "slim Jim" brochures, letterheads, border designs, envelopes, business cards, postcards, mailing labels, and other paper products. You can also purchase paper supplies in sets that include all of the above items in a single design for consistency and cost savings.

Other mail order office suppliers include Quill Corporation (708-634-8000), Moore Business Products (800-323-6230), The Drawing Board (800-527-9530), and The Stationery House (800-638-3033).

If you want to know more about paper selection, get a copy of *Pocket Pal,* published by International Paper, from your paper supplier, the publisher (77 W. 45th St., New York NY 10036), or from The Printers Shopper (111 Press Lane, Chula Vista CA 91910; 800-854-2911). The Printers Shopper sells supplies to print shops and graphics studios. Their catalog includes printing and binding equipment for small printers and desktop publishers.

Desktop Publishing Product Suppliers

Desktop publishing is a growing business. Besides the above resources, there are suppliers who specialize in equipment and software for the desktop publishing industry. They include Publishing Perfection (P.O. Box 307, Menomonee Falls WI 53051; 800-710-5000), Publisher's Toolbox (8845 S. Greenview Dr., Suite 8, Middleton WI 53562; 800-233-3898), and PrePRESS DIRECT (11 Mt. Pleasant Ave., East Hanover NJ 07936; 800-443-6600).

Small Business Administration Resources

Founded over 40 years ago, the U.S. Small Business Administration or SBA (1441 L Street N.W., Washington, DC 20416) has offices in 100 cities across the U.S. and a mandate to help small businesses start and grow. The SBA offers counseling, booklets on business topics, and administers a small business loan guarantee program. To find your area's SBA office, check the white pages of metropolitan telephone books in your region under "United States Government, Small Business Administration."

The SBA also operates the Small Business Answer Desk, a toll-free response line (800-827-5722) that answers questions about SBA services. In addition, it sponsors the 13,000 Service Corps of Retired Executives (SCORE) volunteers, Active Corps of Executives (ACE) volunteers, Business Development Centers, and Technology Access Centers.

The SBA offers a numerous publications, services, and videotapes for starting and managing a small business. Publications are available on products/ideas/inventions, financial management, management and planning, marketing, crime prevention, personnel management, and other topics. The booklets can be purchased for $1 or $2 each at SBA offices or from SBA Publications, P.O. Box 30, Denver CO 80201. Ask first for SBA Form 115A, The Small Business Directory, that lists available publications and includes an order form.

The Service Corps of Retired Executives or SCORE, (1441 L Street N.W./Room 100, Washington DC 20416) is a national nonprofit association with a goal of helping small business. SCORE is sponsored by the SBA and the local SCORE office is usually in or near the SBA office. SCORE and ACE members donate their time and experience to counseling individuals in small business.

Business Development Centers (BDCs) are regional centers funded by the SBA and managed in conjunction with regional colleges. A BDC offers free and confidential counseling for small business owners and managers, new businesses, home-based businesses, and people with business ideas including retail, service, wholesale, manufacturing, and farm businesses. BDCs sponsor seminars on various business topics, assist in developing business and marketing plans, inform entrepreneurs of employer requirements, and teach cash-flow budgeting and management. BDCs also gather information sources, assist in locating business resources, and make referrals.

Small Business Institutes are partnerships between the SBA and nearly 500 colleges and offer counseling services to area businesses. SBIs conduct market research, develop business and marketing plans, and help small businesses work out manufacturing problems. Contact your regional SBA office to find out if a local college has such a program. You could get free or low-cost assistance from the college's business faculty and students.

Tax Information Resources

The U.S. Treasury Department's Internal Revenue Service offers numerous Small Business Tax Education Program videos through its regional offices. Topics include depreciation, business use of your home, employment taxes, excise taxes, starting a business, sole proprietorships, partnerships, self-employed retirement plans, S corporations, and federal tax deposits.

If you're considering using a portion of your home as a business office, request Business Use of Your Home (Publication 587) from the Internal Revenue Service (Washington DC 20224). It's free and will help you determine if your business qualifies for this option, as well as how to take advantage of it to lower your taxes.

Depending on how much you use your business vehicle for personal use, you can either list all costs of operating the vehicle as an expense or you can deduct a standard mileage rate as an expense when you file income taxes. For more information, request Business Use of a Car (Publication 917) from the Internal Revenue Service. There's no charge for this publication.

What business expenses are deductible? There's a long list. The best answer is found in a free publication offered by the Internal Revenue Service, *Business Expenses*. Ask for Publication 535.

To begin your payroll system, contact the Internal Revenue Service (Washington DC 20224) and request the *Employer's Tax Guide* (Circular E) and get a nine-digit Employer Identification Number. The IRS will then send you deposit slips (Form 8109) with your new ID number printed on them. Use these deposit slips each time you pay your payroll taxes. Payroll taxes are paid within a month of the ending of a quarter; that is, January 31, April 30, July 31, and October 31. As your business grows, you may be required to pay payroll taxes more frequently. By then, your accountant will help you determine need and the process.

Action Guidelines

There is a wide variety of resources available to professional desktop publishers, including your experiences, prospective customers, trade associations, conventions, seminars, training courses, books, magazines, suppliers, and governmental offices. Here's how to put them to work for you.

✔ Review your own experiences with successful documents as well as the experiences of friends and family.

✔ Make notes in your desktop publishing notebook on what you feel your prospective customers need and want from a desktop publishing service.

✔ Start calling and writing for catalogs and information from resources.

✔ Review your list of skills and needs, then find training resources to enhance them.

✔ Contact franchisors to determine costs and benefits of buying a franchise or opportunity.

✔ Contact your regional SBA and BDC offices to learn how they can help you start and build your business.

✔ Contact the IRS for booklets, forms, and other resources.

STARTING UP YOUR DESKTOP PUBLISHING SERVICE

Are you ready? By now, you've learned what a successful desktop publishing service does, studied the resources available to you, and decided that you want to start your own desktop publishing service. You're anxious to put your sign out and start producing your first documents.

Not yet. Before you start your desktop publishing service you must first plan to make it a success. You don't want to close up shop in six months because you misjudged the local market or overspent your income. Instead, you want to celebrate your first anniversary looking back on a successful year and looking forward to many more.

This chapter will help you plan for your success and execute that plan to ensure that your desktop publishing business will be profitable.

How to Plan for Your Desktop Publishing Service's Success

The adage that businesses don't plan to fail, they just fail to plan is accurate. Without a plan for your business, you may soon find yourself in a venture that neither satisfies your needs nor pays your bills.

A business plan is a document that can be used both by people contemplating going into business and those already in business. A business plan helps you focus your thoughts and ideas, summarizing your product, your process, your market, and your expectations into a single document that can guide you in your daily decisions as well as help you develop financing for startup and expansion.

An excellent guide for creating a successful business plan is David H. Bang's, Jr. *The Business Planning Guide*, sixth edition (Upstart Publishing). It offers clear, step-by-step procedures for pulling a business plan together for a desktop publishing service or any other business venture. It includes worksheets, resources, and a sample business plan.

If your business plan is intended to develop financing through a bank or a backer, it must also answer the question: How will the funds be repaid?

Your business plan will include a statement of purpose, an outline of your service, a discussion of your customers and

---

Your business plan will answer these five questions:

1. How much money do I need?
2. On what will the money be spent?
3. Who will own and who will operate the business?
4. What are the projected financial results of the company?
5. Do I really know enough about this business?

how you will reach them, as well as current and projected financial information.

A typical desktop publishing service may develop a statement of purpose that reads:

> ABC Desktop Publishing Service will offer cost-effective desktop publishing services to small businesses and advertising agencies in the Midtown district. Startup requires $10,000 in cash from savings for equipment, rent, supplies, and a salary for the first two months of operation until the business is expected to be profitable.

If you're using the business plan to get financing, it will be more detailed and specific than the plan you would write to guide yourself through the first year of operation. In addition, a business plan for a $10,000 startup is typically shorter than one for a $100,000 expansion project.

How to Select Your Business Name

Naming a business is much like naming a baby. In some ways, it will give direction to its growth. A well-named business will seem more successful to prospects, and will then become so.

A business name should make it clear to prospects what the firm does, or at least the industry the firm is in. Here are some examples:

- Midtown Desktop Publishing Service (denotes the location and the product).
- Sandra's Desktop Designs (identifies the product, but is personalized at the expense of sounding like a small business).
- Henderson Publishing Services, Inc. (sounds bigger; surnames are better than first names and incorporation implies that it is a larger firm).

- ABC Newsletter Service (specifically identifies the service and assures early-listing in alphabetical directories such as Yellow Pages).
- Smithtown Services (unclear what service is involved).
- Quality Desktop Publishing Service (clearly identifies the product and the owner's attitude).

In selecting a business name, many firms write a defining motto or slogan that's used in all stationery and advertisements to further clarify what the firm does:

- Specializing in brochures for businesses that want to be busy
- Specializing in low-cost sales collateral
- Desktop Publishing and Printing Services
- Professionally Designed for Results!
- Overnight Service
- Satisfaction Guaranteed
- Since 1975
- Your One-Stop Desktop Publishing Service

An assumed business name is a name other than the real and true name of each person operating a business. A real and true name becomes an assumed business name with the addition of any words that imply the existence of additional owners. For example, *Bob Smith* is a real and true name, while *Bob Smith Company* is an assumed business name.

In most states and counties, you must register an assumed business name to let the public know who is transacting business under that name. Without the registration you may be fined or, worse, not be able to defend a legal action because your assumed business name wasn't properly registered.

In many states, an assumed business name is registered with the state's corporate division. Some states will also register your assumed business name with counties in which you do business. Other states require that you do so. In some locations, you must publish a public notice in an area newspaper telling all that you (and any other business principals) are operating under a specific business name.

The typical assumed business name registration requires the following information: the business name you wish to assume, the principal place of business, the name of an authorized representative, your SIC (standard industrial classification) code, a list of all owners with their signatures, and a list of all counties in which your firm will transact business (sell, lease, or purchase goods or services; receive funding or credit). The SIC for a desktop publishing service is 5734-03.

Where to Locate Your Business

Where will you locate your desktop publishing service? The answer depends on how much business you expect to initially earn, what your space requirements are, your budget, and whether you plan to have clients visit your place of business.

Here are some points to consider as you decide where to locate your business:

- Proximity to your primary clients
- Opportunities for signage
- Availability of transportation
- Requirements and availability of parking facilities
- Cost of operation
- Tax burden
- Quality of police and fire services

- Environmental factors
- Physical suitability of building
- Opportunities for future expansion
- Personal convenience

The first and most important consideration is making sure that you are located conveniently for your clients. The best locations for desktop publishing services are small business offices and retail stores in major business districts, depending on your primary clientele.

Considering these factors, let's look at your options.

Considering a Home Office

About 60 percent of all desktop publishing services operate exclusively from their home. Many others start at home and move to business offices as they grow. The entrepreneur sets up a small office at the dining table, in a walk-in closet, an extra bedroom, or a shop. This is an ideal situation for a part-time desktop publishing service for many reasons. First, there will be little or no additional rent expense. It is also more convenient for you to have all your records at home, where you can review them at any time. In addition, you could have a family member or someone living with you help by answering the telephone while you're away. Finally, you can legally deduct some of your household costs as legitimate expenses and reduce your tax obligation.

But the best reason is that it saves you time. A client can call you in the evening to ask about a specific job and you can quickly check your records or make notes in the job file without leaving your home. The most popular initial location for a home-based desktop publishing service is a desk in a spare room.

Of course, with a home office, you will want to discourage walk-in customers. Don't include your address in your ads.

Rather, have prospects call to set up an appointment. Make sure that the path from your front door to your office is short and looks as professional as possible. Customers are hiring you for your professionalism as well as your desktop production skills.

Considering a Shared Office

You may have friends or relatives who own a related service business, such as a print shop. You could share an office with them, reducing your costs and bringing them some rental income. Of course, don't share an office with anyone who may, in any way, be a competitor or be associated with a competitor. Prospects calling for you could be diverted.

The most common structure for renting a shared office is to pay a portion of the utility bills and a percentage of all sales you make. Have an attorney draw up your agreement to ensure that it is legally binding on both parties.

Considering Your Own Office

As your desktop publishing service business grows, you will want to move to your own office. The biggest disadvantage of such a move is the cost. But there are many advantages. First, your own office will give you an image of being a large, successful, and permanent firm. Second, your business requires that prospects, clients, or others come to your office. An office of your own will give them a better first impression. Third, it will give you control over your business that you cannot have if you're working out of a spare bedroom or a shared office.

Many desktop publishing services prefer to locate in professional office centers with other services for the business community: attorneys, business consultants, copy shops, résumé services. Especially consider professional office centers with well-known tenants that will encourage foot traffic.

Considering a Shopping Mall

Desktop publishing services typically don't locate in a shopping mall because of the high costs. However, many take advantage of the mall's traffic by renting a professional office on a mall's second floor or in a satellite office complex next to a popular mall. There are many types of shopping malls: neighborhood, community, regional, and super-regional.

A neighborhood shopping center is built around a supermarket or drugstore with a trade population of 2,500 to 40,000 and offers 30,000 to 100,000 square feet of leasable space.

A community shopping center (100,000 to 300,000 square feet) often has a variety or discount department store as its leading tenant and serves a trade population of 40,000 to 150,000.

A regional shopping center (300,000 to 1,000,000 square feet) builds around one or more full-line department stores with a trade population of 150,000 or more.

A super-regional shopping center includes three or more department stores with more than 750,000 square feet of leasable space.

Selecting the Right Location

The old business adage says that the three most important factors in selecting a retail site are: location, location, and location. The most important aspect of location is retail compatibility. For your small store in its first years of operation, with limited funds for advertising and promotion, locating your store near a traffic-generator can help you survive. You'll often find restaurants grouped together. Competing antique stores may take over a city block.

The next most important factor in selecting your retail site is the availability of a local merchants association. A strong merchants association can accomplish through group strength what an individual store owner couldn't even dream of. Not only can a merchants association speak as a booming voice to city planners, it can also bulk-buy advertising at lower rates to promote its own events. But make sure that you understand your responsibilities to the association before you sign up. If the site you select doesn't have a merchants association, consider starting one.

Other factors include the responsiveness of the landlord and the opportunities for negotiating a favorable lease. Make sure your new landlord is continuing an investment in the property, including regular maintenance and quick repairs. And talk with other commercial landlords in your area to ensure that your lease is the best you can negotiate.

You can often get assistance on selecting a retail site by talking with local and regional chambers of commerce about your needs. They may be able to give you an educated guess on what you will probably have to pay to lease a property that will help your business become successful.

Checking Zoning Laws

Your desktop publishing location may be limited by local zoning laws. Before deciding where you will set up your business, talk to the local zoning office about restrictions. You may find that so-called cottage or home businesses are allowed in your neighborhood as long as clients don't park on the street.

The Americans with Disabilities Act (ADA) assures employees and customers in many firms access to business locations without physical barriers. The ADA requires that business owners offer easy access that does not restrict people with disabilities from entering their premises. This act applies to all businesses with 15 or more employees. To learn more about ADA requirements, contact the Small Business Research and Education Council (800-947-4646).

Understanding Employment Laws

If you decide to add employees to your desktop publishing service, there are certain laws, federal and state, that come into play. Your local state employment office can assist you in learning the current requirements of these laws.

The Social Security Act of 1935, as amended, is concerned with employment insurance laws as well as retirement insurance.

The Fair Labor Standards Act of 1938, as amended, establishes minimum wages, overtime pay, record keeping, and child labor standards for most businesses.

The Occupational Safety and Health Act (OSHA) of 1970 is concerned with safety and health in the workplace and covers almost all employers. There are specific standards, regulations, and reporting requirements that must be met.

There are other laws that may concern your business. Contact your local state employment office to determine the requirements for hiring disadvantaged workers, federal service contracts for work on public buildings or other public projects, employee pension and welfare benefit plans, and the garnishment of employees' wages.

In addition, the Immigration Reform and Control Act of 1986 prohibits employing illegal aliens. Employers must require every employee to fill out the Employment Eligibility Verification Form (Form 19) within three days of the date of hire (if hired after November 7, 1987). Fines are levied for noncompliance. For more information, contact the nearest office of the Immigration and Naturalization Service.

The Civil Rights Act of 1964 prohibits discrimination in employment practices because of race, religion, sex, or national origin. Public Law 90-202 prohibits discrimination on the basis of age with respect to individuals who are between 40 and 70 years of age. Federal laws also prohibit discrimination against the physically handicapped. Again, your state employment office can help you in understanding the laws regarding applicants and employment. In addition, firms like G. Neil (720 International Parkway, Sunrise FL 33345) offer catalogs of human relations supplies: job applications, personnel folders, labor law posters, attendance controllers, employee awards, and related materials.

Selecting the Right Business Form

One of the most important decisions you will make as you start your desktop publishing service is what legal form it will take. Why so important? Because how you record expenses, how you build your business, how you pay taxes, how you treat profits, and how you manage liability all depend on the structure you give your business.

Of course, as your business grows you'll be able to move from one type of structure to another, but sometimes there will be a cost. The cost will be paid to the tax man, as he decides whether you changed structure to avoid paying your fair share of taxes. One of the reasons you may later change structure is because you want to legally reduce tax liability—and that's OK. It's the abuse of tax laws that brings the wrath of the IRS.

There are three common types of business structures: proprietorship, partnership, and corporation. Each has specific advantages and disadvantages, but they must all be considered against your individual circumstances, goals, and needs.

Proprietorship

A sole proprietorship is a business that is owned and operated by one person. However, in many states a business owned jointly by a husband and wife is considered a proprietorship, rather than a partnership. Proprietorship is the easiest form of business to establish. In most locations, you only need to obtain required licenses and begin operation. For its simplicity, the proprietorship is the most widespread form of small business organization and is especially popular with new desktop publishers.

The first and most obvious advantage of a proprietorship is ease of formation. There is less formality and fewer legal restrictions associated with establishing a sole proprietorship. It needs little or no governmental approval and is less expensive to start than a partnership or a corporation.

Another advantage of a proprietorship is that you don't have to share profits with anyone. Whatever is left over after you pay the bills (including taxes) is yours to keep. You will report income, expenses, and profit to the IRS, using Schedule C and your standard 1040 form, and make quarterly estimated tax payments to the IRS so you don't get behind before your annual filing.

Control is important to the successful desktop publishing service. A proprietorship gives that control and decision-making power to a single person, you. Proprietorships also give the owner flexibility that other forms of business do not. A partner must usually get agreement from other partners. In larger matters, a corporation must get agreement from other members of the board of directors or corporate officers. A proprietor simply makes up his or her mind and acts.

One more plus—the sole proprietor has relative freedom from government control and special taxation. Sure, the government has some say in how you operate and what taxes you will pay. But the government has less to say to the sole proprietor.

Yes, there's a downside to being the only boss. Most important is unlimited liability. The individual proprietor is responsible for the full amount of business debts, which may exceed the proprietor's total investment. With some exceptions, this liability extends to all the proprietor's assets, such as house and car. One way around this is for the proprietor to obtain sufficient insurance coverage to reduce the risk from physical loss and personal injury. But if you aren't paying your suppliers, they can come after your assets.

When the business is a single individual, the serious illness or death of that person can end the business.

Individuals typically cannot get the credit and capital that partnerships and corporations can. Fortunately, most desktop publishing service don't require extensive capital. But when they do, they seriously consider the advantages of taking on a partner or becoming a corporation.

Finally, as a sole proprietor your business receives your relatively limited viewpoint and experience. You're more subject to tunnel vision or seeing things in a narrow way based on your experiences. You don't have someone with a commitment to your business who can give you a fresh viewpoint or new ideas.

Partnership

The Uniform Partnership Act (UPA) adopted by many states defines a partnership as "an association of two or more persons to carry on as co-owners of a business for profit." How the partnership is structured, the powers and limitations of each partner, and their participation in the business are written into a document called the Articles of Partnership. The articles or descriptions can either be written by the partners, found in a legal form from a stationery store, or written by an attorney. Obviously, using an attorney is the best option because it ensures that the document is binding, and reduces the likelihood of disputes that typically come up once the business is growing.

A partnership can typically raise capital more easily than a proprietorship. This is because there are more people whose assets can be combined as equity for the loan. Lenders will look at the credit ratings of each partner, so make sure that your business partners have good credit.

Your firm's Articles of Partnership should include:

- the name, location, length, and purpose of the partnership;
- the type of partnership;
- a definition of the partners' individual contributions;
- an agreement on how business expenses will be handled;
- an outline of the authority of each partner;
- a summary of the accounting methods that will be used;
- definition of how profits and losses will be distributed among the partners;
- the salaries and capital draws for each partner;
- an agreement of how the partnership will be modified or terminated, including dissolution of the partnership by death or disability of a member or by the decision of partners to disband; and
- a description of how the members will arbitrate and settle disputes as well as change terms of the partnership agreement.

Partnerships are easier and less costly to form than corporations. In most states, all that's really needed is Articles of Partnership.

Partnerships are frequently more flexible in the decision-making process than a corporation, but less flexible than a proprietorship, as discussed earlier.

And, like proprietorships, partnerships offer relative freedom from government control and special taxation. A partnership usually doesn't pay income tax. Rather, all profits and losses flow through the partnership to the individual partners, who pay income and other taxes as if they were sole proprietors.

Of course, there are some minuses to partnerships. Like sole proprietorships, at least one partner will be a general partner and will assume unlimited liability for the business. Obtain sufficient insurance coverage to reduce the risk from physical loss or personal injury. But the general partner is still liable.

A partnership is as stable or as unstable as its members. Elimination of any partner often means automatic dissolution of the partnership. However, the business can continue to operate if the agreement includes provisions for the right of survivorship and possible creation of a new partnership. Partnership insurance can assist surviving partners in purchasing the equity of a deceased partner.

Though a partnership has less difficulty in getting financing than a sole proprietorship, the fragile nature of partnerships sometimes makes it difficult to get long-term financing. The best strategy, as discussed earlier, is using the combined equity of the partners from assets they own as individuals. In fact, many partnerships are started because an active partner needs equity or financing that he cannot get without a partner with more assets or better credit.

Depending upon how the partnership agreement is drawn, any partner may be able to bind all of the partners to financial obligations. Make sure your Articles of Partnership accurately reflects your intent regarding how partners can or cannot obligate the partnership.

A major drawback to partnerships is the difficulty faced when a partner leaves the business. Buying out the partner's interest may be difficult unless terms have been specifically worked out in the partnership agreement.

As you can see, there are numerous pluses and minuses to partnerships. Many of the disadvantages can be taken care of in your Articles of Partnership. It is recommended that you use an attorney experienced in such agreements as you construct your partnership. The value usually exceeds the cost.

Corporation

Businesses, as they grow, often become corporations, identified by an extension to their name: Corp., Inc., or, in Canada, Ltd. A corporation is usually formed by the authority of a state government. The steps to forming a corporation begin with writing incorporation papers and issuing capital stock. Then, approval must be obtained from the Secretary of State in the state in which the corporation is being formed. Only then can the corporation act as a legal entity separate from those who own its stock.

The primary advantage to incorporation is that it limits the stockholders' liability to their investment. If you buy $1,000 of stock in a corporation that fails, you can only lose up to the $1,000 investment. The corporation's creditors cannot come back to you demanding more money. The exception is when you put up some of your own assets as collateral for the corporation.

Ownership of a corporation is a transferable asset. The New York Stock Exchange and other exchanges make a big business out of transferring stock or partial ownership in corporations from one investor to another. If your desktop publishing service is a corporation, you can sell partial ownership or stock in it within certain limits. In fact, this is how many corporations get money to grow. A corporation can also issue long-term bonds to gain cash required to purchase assets or build the business.

Your corporation has a separate and legal existence. Your corporation is not you or anybody else. It is itself. For example, in the case of illness, death, or other cause for loss of a corporate officer or owner, the corporation continues to exist and do business.

The corporation can also delegate authority to hired managers, although they are often one and the same. Thus you become an employee of the corporation.

Corporations have disadvantages, too. The corporation's state charter may limit the type of business to a specific industry or service. However, other states allow broad charters that permit corporations to operate in any legal enterprise.

Corporations face more governmental regulations on all levels: local, state, and federal. An incorporated business will spend more time and money fulfilling requirements to which a proprietorship or a partnership is not subject.

In addition, if your corporate manager is not also a stockholder, he will have less incentive to be efficient than he would if he had a share in your business.

As you can imagine, a corporation is more expensive to form than other types of businesses. Even if you don't use an attorney, there are forms and fees that will quickly add up. However, an attorney is a good investment when incorporating your desktop publishing business.

Finally, corporations allow the federal and some state governments to tax income twice: once as the corporate net income and once as it's received by the individual stockholders in the form of salary or dividends. A Sub-Chapter S corporation allows small businesses to tax the business as if it were a proprietorship or partnership, (no income tax) and the tax liability passes directly to the individual stockholders without corporate income tax. Talk with an attorney and/or accountant about this option.

Hiring an Attorney

To find an attorney who is familiar with business of your size and trade, ask for a referral from a business colleague, your banker, your accountant, your local chamber of commerce, or other businesses in your area. Many local bar associations run an attorney referral and information service; check your local telephone book's Yellow Pages under LAWYERS' REFERRAL & INFORMATION SERVICES. Some referral services give you only names and phone numbers; others actually give information on experience and fees to help you match your needs to the attorney's background and charges.

An attorney can help you decide which is the most advantageous business structure. He or she can also help you with zoning, licensing problems, unpaid bills, contracts and agreements, employment laws, copyright questions, trademarks, and some tax problems.

Because there is always the possibility of a lawsuit, claim, or other legal action against your business, it is wise to have an attorney who is already familiar with your business before a crisis arises.

Let your attorney know that you expect to be informed of all developments and consulted before any decisions are made on your behalf. You may also want to request copies of all documents, letters, and memos written and received regarding your project. If this isn't practical, you should at least have the opportunity to read such correspondence at your attorney's office.

Hiring an Accountant

Many new desktop publishing services fail because of poor financial management. Sometimes the best decision a new business owner makes is to hire the services of a public accounting firm. An accountant can set up a record-keeping system and ways for maintaining it, as well as help you access vital information and relate it to profitability.

Daily bits of information will flow into your desktop publishing service. Transactions will generate information about sales, cash, supplies, purchase expenses, payroll, accounts payable, and, if credit is offered to customers, accounts receivable.

To capture these facts and figures, a system is necessary. If you don't feel comfortable with setting up and managing such a system, don't be shy about hiring an accounting service.

Once you've established a system of records, the question is: Who should keep the books? The accounting service that set up the books may keep them. However, if you have a general understanding of record keeping, you can do them yourself and save some money. Use your accountant for checking and analyzing your records. Once your business has grown, you may want to hire someone to keep your records and perform other office functions.

In addition to record keeping, an accountant can advise you on financial management, such as cash flow requirements, budget forecasts, borrowing, business organization, and tax information.

To help you on cash flow requirements, an accountant will work out the amount of cash needed to operate your firm during a specific period—for example, three months, six months, the next year. He or she considers how much cash you will need to carry customer accounts receivable, to buy equipment and supplies, to pay current bills, and to repay loans. In addition, an accountant can determine how much cash will come from collection of accounts receivable and how much will have to be borrowed or pulled from an existing line of credit. While working out the cash requirements, your accountant may notice and call your attention to danger spots such as accounts that are past due.

When you apply for a loan, your accountant can assemble financial information, such as a profit-and-loss or income statement and a balance sheet. The purpose of such data is to show the lender the financial position of your business and its ability to repay the loan. Using this information, your accountant can advise you on whether you need a short-term or long-term loan. If you have never borrowed before, your accountant may help by introducing you to a lender who knows and respects the accountant's reputation. This alone may be worth the cost of hiring an accountant.

Taxes are another area in which an accountant can contribute advice and assistance. Normally, a record-keeping system that provides the information you need for making profitable decisions will suffice for tax purposes. However, if you purchase a lot of equipment that requires special depreciation, your employees handle cash or require payroll taxes, or you have extensive bad debts, a good accountant can help you identify the problems, suggest a method of keeping good records, and help you minimize your tax obligation by writing off bad debts as a business expense.

In looking for an accountant, get referrals from trusted friends, business associations, professional associations, and other business services. Discuss fees in advance and draw up a written agreement about how you will work together.

To summarize potential services: your accountant can advise on initial business decisions, help you set up your records, prepare and analyze income statements, advise on financial decisions involving the purchase of capital assets, and advise on cash requirements for the successful continuation of your venture. He or she can make budget forecasts, help prepare financial information for a loan application, and handle tax matters. Accounting firms will also obtain your federal and state withholding numbers, instruct on where and when to file tax returns, prepare tax returns, and do general tax planning for your small business.

Your accountant is your key financial adviser. He or she should alert you to potential danger areas and advise you on how to handle growth spurts, how to best plan for slow business times, and how to financially mature and protect your business future from unnecessary risk.

Hiring an Insurance Agent

A good insurance agent is as valuable to your success as any other professional consultant. A good insurance agent can minimize your exposure to risk, while keeping your insurance costs reasonable.

As with other advisors, ask around among other business services and professionals for recommendations of a good insurance agent. If possible, search for one who primarily serves the business community, rather than the family or individuals. They will better know your problems and concerns.

Ask prospective agents for some advice on a specific problem. Don't tell them what you think the solution is. Their response can help you determine who is the best at cost-effective problem solving.

The agent is the insurance industry's primary client representative. Typically, the independent agent is a small business owner and manager. By using this distribution system, insurance companies are represented by agents who receive a commission for selling the companies' products and services. An independent agent may represent more than one insurance company.

Liability insurance coverages, particularly for property damage and bodily injury, usually include legal defense at no additional charge when the policyholder is named a party to the lawsuit that involves a claim covered by the policy. Litigation is costly, whether the claimant's suit is valid or frivolous. The legal defense provision greatly reduces these costs to you.

Action Guidelines

Starting your desktop publishing service requires a number of important steps: testing your business idea, estimating start-up costs, selecting your business name, locating your business, choosing the form of your business, and selecting your professional advisors. Here's how to implement what you've learned in Chapter 4.

- ✔ Start writing your business plan. Refer to *The Business Planning Guide* and other resources for worksheets and examples.
- ✔ Write your business's statement of purpose.
- ✔ Select your business name and find out how to register and protect it.
- ✔ Develop a slogan or motto that best fits your business.
- ✔ Decide where to initially locate your business. Research and consider many locations, writing information in your desktop publishing business notebook.
- ✔ Contact your state employment office and other government offices regarding employment laws and requirements.
- ✔ Decide which form of business you will initially use: proprietorship, partnership, or corporation.
- ✔ Find a good attorney.
- ✔ Find a good accountant.
- ✔ Find a good insurance agent.

Chapter 5

OPERATING YOUR DESKTOP PUBLISHING SERVICE

Starting a new business is only part of your goal. To succeed you must manage its day-to-day operation. You must control operating costs, keep and analyze records, price and produce effective documents, hire and manage employees, and pay taxes.

This chapter covers these and other responsibilities for your desktop publishing service's daily operations as suggested by successful business persons. It will help you understand and focus on the nuts and bolts of your business as you keep your eyes on the broader purpose of your venture—to help others as you help yourself.

How to Estimate Operating Costs

Managing your desktop publishing service requires that you manage your business budget, so you can continue to provide service, support, and employment to others as well as a profit to yourself. When you first started your business, you established a preliminary budget. Now that your business is operating, you must establish an operating budget.

A budget is a forecast of all cash sources and cash expenditures. It is organized in the same format as a financial statement, and most commonly covers a 12-month period. At the end of the year, the anticipated income and expenses developed in the budget are compared to the actual performance of the business as recorded in the financial statement.

A budget can greatly enhance your chances of success by helping you estimate future needs and plan profits, spending, and overall cash flow. A budget allows you to detect problems before they occur and to alter your plans to prevent those problems.

In business, budgets help you determine how much money you have and how you will use it, as well as help you decide whether you have enough money to achieve your financial goals. As part of your business plan, a budget can help convince a loan officer that you know your business and have anticipated its needs.

A budget will indicate the cash required for necessary labor and materials, day-to-day operating costs, revenue needed to support business operations, and expected profit. If your budget indicates that you need more revenue than you can earn, you can adjust your plans by:

- reducing expenditures (hiring part-time rather than full-time employees, purchasing less expensive furniture, eliminating an extra telephone line),
- expanding sales (offering additional services, conducting an aggressive marketing campaign, hiring a salesperson), or
- lowering your salary or profit expectations.

There are three main elements to a budget: sales revenue, total costs, and profit.

Sales revenue is the cornerstone of a budget. It is crucial to project sales as accurately as possible. Base estimates on actual past sales figures. Once you target sales, you can calculate the related expenses necessary to achieve your goals.

Total costs include fixed and variable costs. Estimating costs is complicated because you must identify which costs will change—and by how much—and which costs will remain unchanged as sales increase. You must also consider inflation and rising prices as appropriate.

Variable costs vary directly with sales. Paper and printer toner expenses are examples of variable costs for your desktop publishing service. Fixed costs don't change regardless of sales volume. Rent is considered a fixed cost, as are salaries. Semi variable costs, such as telephone expenses, have both variable and fixed components. So part of the expense is listed as fixed (telephone line charges) and part is variable (long distance charges).

Profit should be large enough to make a return on cash investment and a return on your work. Your investment is the money you put into the firm at start-up and the profit of prior years you left in the firm (retained earnings). If you can receive 10 percent interest on $10,000 by investing outside of your business, then you should expect a similar return when investing $10,000 in equipment and other assets within the business. In targeting profits, you also want to be sure you're receiving a fair return on your labor. Your weekly paycheck should be consistent with what you could be earning elsewhere as an employee.

How to Establish an Operating Budget

As you develop your budget, you'll be working with the budget equation. The basic budget equation is:

$$\text{Sales} = \text{Total Costs} + \text{Profit}$$

This equation shows that every sales dollar you receive is made up partly of a recovery of your costs and partly of profit. Another way to express the basic budgeting equation is:

$$\text{Sales - Total Costs = Profit}$$

This equation shows that, after reimbursing yourself for the cost of producing your service, the remaining part of the sales dollar is profit. For example, if you expect $1,000 for a specific job, and you know that it will cost $900 to market and perform this service, your profit will be $100.

In calculating an operating budget, you will often make estimates based on past sales and cost figures. You will need to adjust these figures to reflect price increases, inflation, and other factors. For example, for the past three years, a desktop publisher spent an average of $1,500 on advertising costs per year. For the coming year, the owner expects an advertising cost increase of 5 percent (0.05). To calculate next year's advertising costs, the owner multiplies the average annual advertising costs by the percentage price increase ($1,500 x 0.05 = $75) and adds that amount to the original annual cost ($1,500 + $75 = $1,575). A shortcut method is to multiply the original advertising cost by one plus the rate of increase ($1,500 x 1.05 = $1,575).

If your desktop publishing service is a new venture and has no past financial records, rely on your own experience and knowledge of the industry to estimate demand for and costs of your service, such as the income and profit potentials provided in Chapter 1 of this book. Your accountant or trade association can also help you develop realistic estimates.

Before you create an operating budget, you must answer three questions:

1. How much net profit do you realistically want your business to generate during the calendar year?

2. How much will it cost to produce that profit?
3. How much sales revenue is necessary to support both profit and cost requirements?

To answer these questions, consider expected sales and all costs, either direct or indirect, associated with your desktop publishing service. To make the safest estimates when budgeting, most companies prefer to overestimate expenses and underestimate sales revenue.

Start constructing your budget with either a forecast of sales or a forecast of profits. For practical purposes, most small businesses start with a forecast of profits. In other words, decide what profit you realistically want to make and then list the expenses you will incur to make that profit.

How to Keep Good Records

Why keep records?

There are many reasons. For the individual just starting a desktop publishing service, an adequate record-keeping system increases the chances of survival. In addition, established desktop publishing services can enhance the chances of staying in business and earning increased profits with a good record-keeping system.

Keeping accurate and up-to-date business records is, for many people, the most difficult and uninteresting aspect of operating a business. If this area of business management is one that you believe will be hard for you, plan now how you will handle this task. Don't wait until tax time or until you're totally confused. Take a course at a local community college, ask a volunteer SCORE representative, or hire an accountant to advise you on setting up and maintaining you record-keeping system.

Your records will be used to prepare tax returns, make business decisions, and apply for loans. Set aside a special time

Here are some questions that good business records can answer:
- How much business am I doing?
- How much credit am I extending?
- How are my collections?
- What are my losses from credit sales?
- Who owes me money?
- Who is delinquent?
- Should I continue extending credit to delinquent accounts?
- How much cash do I have on hand?
- How much cash do I have in the bank?
- Does this amount agree with what records tell me I should have, or is there a shortage?
- How much is my investment in equipment?
- How often do I turn over my supplies inventory?
- How much do I owe my suppliers and other creditors?
- How much gross profit or margin did I earn?
- What were my expenses?
- What's my weekly payroll?
- Do I have adequate payroll records to meet the requirements of workers' compensation insurance, wage-and-hour laws, social security insurance, unemployment compensation insurance, and withholding taxes?
- How much net profit did I earn last month?
- How much income taxes will I owe?
- Are my sales, expenses, profits, and capital showing improvements or did I do better last year than this?
- How do I stand as compared with two periods ago?
- Is my business's position about the same, improving, or deteriorating?
- On what services am I making a profit, breaking even, or losing money?
- Am I taking full advantage of cash discounts for prompt payments?
- How do my discounts taken compare with my discounts given?
- How do the financial facts of my desktop publishing service compare with those of similar businesses?

Get the point? Your business requires a good record-keeping system to help you work smarter rather than harder.

each day to update your records. It will pay off in the long run with more deductions and fewer headaches.

So what do you need for a good record-keeping or accounting system. A good record-keeping system should be:

- Simple to use
- Easy to understand
- Reliable
- Accurate
- Consistent
- Timely

Several published systems and software systems provide simplified records, usually in a single record book. These systems cover the primary records required for all businesses, some are designed specifically for the desktop publishing service business. Check your local office supply store, your trade association, or trade journals for more information on specialized record books.

Simply, your records should tell you these three facts:

1. How much cash you owe
2. How much cash is owed to you
3. How much cash you have on hand

To keep track of everything, you should have these basic journals:

- A sales journal shows the business transaction, date, for whom it was performed, the amount of the invoice, how much for labor and how much for materials, and any applicable sales tax.
- A cash receipts register shows the amount of money received, from whom, and for what.
- A cash disbursements register or check register shows each check disbursed, the date of the disbursement,

number of the check, to whom it was made out (payee), the amount of money disbursed, and for what purpose.
- A general journal for noncash transactions and those involving the owner's equity in the business.

In addition, here are other records you will need in your business:

- Accounts receivable is the record of accounts for items and services sold for which you have not yet been paid.
- Accounts payable is the record of accounts of products or services you have purchased but for which you have not yet paid in full.
- Inventory is a record of your firm's investment in paper, envelopes, books, and other items you intend to resell.
- Equipment is a record of your firm's investment in equipment that you will use in providing your service and will not normally resell.
- Payroll is a record of the wages of employees and their deductions for income, FICA (Social Security insurance), and other taxes, as well as other payroll deductions.

Some businesses combine all of these journals into a single journal. In fact, there are many good "one-write" systems available that allow you to make a single entry for each transaction.

Understanding Record Systems

There are two ways to record transactions in your business, single entry or double entry. The primary advantage to single entry record keeping is that it is easy. As the name implies, you make a single entry that records the source of each income or destination of each expense. Each entry is either a plus or a minus to the amount of cash that you have. Receipt of a check on an outstanding account is a plus. Payment of a supplies order is a minus. As long as you have a limited number of transactions, single entry accounting is adequate.

But as your desktop publishing service grows in complexity, you will want a check-and-balance system that ensures that records are accurate. Double entry accounting requires that you make two offsetting entries that balance each other. A check received on an outstanding account is a debit to Cash and a credit to Accounts Receivable. Payment for a supplies order is a debit to Supplies and a credit to Cash.

Every account has two sides: a left or debit side and a right or credit side. The posted debits must always equal the posted credits. Some types of accounts are called debit accounts because their balance is typically a debit. Asset accounts (cash, accounts receivable) are debit accounts. Liability accounts (accounts payable, notes payable) usually carry a credit balance. Income carries a credit balance while expenses carry a debit balance.

Everything else within double entry bookkeeping is based on the above rules. Here are some examples of common double entries:

- Cash income = debit cash and credit income
- Credit or accrued income = debit accounts receivable and credit income
- Cash expense = debit the expense account and credit cash
- Credit or accrued expense = debit the expense account and credit accounts payable
- Prepaid expense = debit prepaid expenses and credit cash

If, at the end of the month, the debits don't equal the credits, check for debits erroneously posted as credits, credits erroneously posted as debits, transposition of numbers (such as 123 to 132), and incorrect math.

Understanding Assets, Liabilities, and Net Worth

Assets include not only cash, equipment, inventory, land, building, furniture, and the like, but also accounts receivable, also known as notes receivable.

Liabilities are funds acquired for a business through loans or the sale of property or services to the business on credit. Creditors do not acquire ownership in your business, but hold promissory notes to be paid at a designated future date (known as accounts or notes payable).

Net worth (or shareholders' equity or capital) is money put into a business by its owners or left in it as retained earnings for use by the business in acquiring assets.

The formula for this structure is:

$$\text{Assets} = \text{Liabilities} + \text{Net Worth}$$

That is, the total funds invested in assets of the business is equal to the funds supplied to the business by its creditors plus the funds supplied to the business by its owners. If a business owes more money to creditors than it possesses in value of assets owned and retained earnings, the net worth or owner's equity of the business will be a negative number.

This accounting formula can also be expressed as:

$$\text{Assets} - \text{Liabilities} = \text{Net Worth}$$

Understanding Cash and Accrual Accounting

Many small businesses are operated primarily on a cash basis. The customer buys products with cash, the merchant buys inventory with cash or short-term credit. As businesses become larger and more complicated, many keep records on the accrual basis. The dividing line between cash basis and accrual basis might depend on whether or not credit is given to customers as well as the amount of inventory required.

Accrual basis is a method of recording income and expenses in which each item is reported as earned or incurred, regardless of when actual payments are received or made. Charge sales are credited at once to Sales and charged to Accounts Receivable. When the bills are collected, the credit is to Accounts Receivable.

Accruals should also be made for larger expense items payable in the future, such as annual or semiannual interest on loans.

If you're comfortable with accounting, accrual can be the most accurate basis for records. But the cash basis is easiest to understand. As long as you don't prepay many of your expenses and are not incorporated, a cash basis is fine for your new desktop publishing service.

Managing Accounts Receivable

Income not yet paid to you is called Accounts Receivable. Here are a few rules that can help you keep Accounts Receivable current. First, be sure bills are prepared immediately after the service is performed. And make sure that the statement is mailed to the correct person and address with sufficient information on the statement to fully identify the source and purpose of the charge. Note that some businesses will simply set aside any bills that they question.

At the end of each month, *age* your Accounts Receivable. That is, list accounts and enter the amounts that are current, unpaid for 30 days, and those 60 days or more past due. Most Accounts Receivable computer programs will produce reports on aged receivables. Then call each account in the 60+ days column and find out why the bill is unpaid. Keep an especially close watch on larger accounts.

To ensure that you get paid promptly, pay close attention to customers' complaints about bills. If a complaint is justified, offer an adjustment and reach an agreement with the customer. Then get a date from the customer as to when you can expect to receive the payment.

Managing Payroll Records

Quarterly and yearly reports of individual payroll payments must be made to federal and, in many cases, state governments. Each individual employee must receive a W-2 form by January 31st showing total withholding payments made for the employee during the previous year.

A payroll summary should be made each payday showing the names, employee number, rate of pay, hours worked, overtime hours, total pay, and amount of deductions for FICA, Medicare insurance, state and federal withholding taxes, deductions for insurance, pension, savings, and child support, as required.

To ensure that you maintain adequate records for this task, keep an employee card for each employee of your firm. The employee card or computer file should show the full legal name, social security number, address, telephone number, name of next of kin and their address, marital status, number of exemptions claimed, and current rate of pay. A federal W-4 form completed and signed by the employee should also be attached to the employee card or record.

Also maintain a running total of earnings, pay, and deductions for each individual employee.

In addition, if your business employs union members, you may have additional deductions for union dues, pensions, and other fees.

Managing Petty Cash

Most business expenses will be paid by business check, credit card, or placed on account with the seller. However, there may be some small expenses that will be paid by an employee or with cash that requires reimbursement. Because the amount is typically small, the fund from which the reimbursement comes is usually known as petty cash.

A petty cash fund should be set up to be used for payments of small amounts not covered by invoices. A check should be drawn for, say, $100. The check is cashed, and the funds placed in a box or drawer. When small cash payments are made for such items as postage, shipping, or supplies, the items are listed on a printed form or even a slip of paper. When the fund is nearly exhausted, the items are summarized and a check drawn to cover the exact amount spent. The check is cashed, and the fund replenished. At all times, the cash in the drawer plus the listed expenditures should equal the established amount of the petty cash fund.

Managing Equipment Records

Keep an accurate and up-to-date list of permanent equipment used in your desktop publishing business. Especially, keep track of equipment useful for a year or longer and of significant value. Equipment records should show date purchased, name of seller, description of item, check number of payment(s), and amount of purchase including tax. If you own a number of items, keep a separate list for vehicles, computers and printers, and office furniture and fixtures. From these records you will develop a depreciation worksheet and provide supporting information for fixed asset accounts.

A charge to expenses should be made to cover depreciation of fixed assets other than land. Fixed assets are any item you purchase to use in your business for a year or longer. Examples are buildings, vehicles, equipment, furniture, and office fixtures. Smaller businesses will usually charge depreciation at the end of their fiscal year, but if your business grows and you have major fixed assets you or your accountant may decide to calculate depreciation monthly.

As clarification, a calendar year is 12 consecutive months beginning January 1 and ending December 31. A fiscal year is 12 consecutive months ending on the last day of any month other than December. A short tax year is less than 12 months because your firm was not in business a full year or you have changed your tax year.

Pricing Your Desktop Publishing Services

How much should you charge for your desktop publishing services? How much does the service cost you to furnish? Once you've established your start-up costs and your monthly operating costs, you'll have a good idea of how much your service will cost you to furnish to your customers. But there's one more important factor that you need—your amount of available time.

A month with 20 work days offers you approximately 160 hours of your time that you can sell to customers. You may wind up working more, but 160 is probably all you'll be able to bill to clients. In fact, depending on the size and structure of your business, you may not be able to bill that many. Most one-person desktop publishing businesses require about a quarter of their time to market their services and to manage the business. So you're down to 120 billable hours per month, unless you work extra hours. If the operating or overhead costs calculated earlier total $6,000 a month, that amount is divided by 120 billable hours to come up with an hourly fee of $50. With monthly operating expenses of $4,000 and 160 billable hours in a month, the hourly rate becomes $25. Quite a range—$25 to $50 per hour.

How much are your competitors charging? A few telephone calls should get you the rates charged by your competitors. Of course, you must make sure that you're comparing apples with apples. Your competitor may not have your level of skill in this area, or may have more. Or your competitor may be including costs for some specialized equipment or software you don't have yet. To determine your competitor's hourly rate rather than product price, ask, "If I preferred to pay you by the hour, how much would you charge?"

Why should you care what your competitors charge? Because your clients will probably get bids from them as well. You don't necessarily have to match or beat their bids, but you do need to know what their rates are so that you can help the client make a fair comparison.

How much do your customers expect to pay? Remember that the question isn't how much will the customers pay, it's how much do they expect to pay? The difference is expectations. You may get some customers to pay an excessive fee for awhile, but they'll soon move to other sources. What you want to find out is what they think your service is actually worth to them. Most understand that, if they pay you too little, you will soon be out of business and won't be there able to help them in the future. They may not admit to it, but they know it.

How can you know how much the customer expects to pay for your skills? Ask a few. They may tell you what they're used to paying, what they think is a fair price, or maybe what they wish they were paying. Take them all into consideration. Ask the question of them, and let them take a few minutes explain why they think so. You'll get some valuable insight into what customers expect from you, as well as what you should expect from them.

As before, make sure that you're comparing similar skills and similar fees. A customer may expect more skills than you can offer—or maybe fewer.

Establishing your hourly service rate is a simple process of adding overhead and expected profit to the cost of labor. If you want to pay yourself $20 per hour and a benefits package worth $6 per hour, add to this your overhead, which is, say, $10 an hour and your expected profit, such as 10 percent of the labor/benefits/overhead cost or $5. You come up with a total of about $40 per hour.

You then apply this hourly rate to the work you do. If a four-page newsletter takes you one hour for the design and two more hours to produce, you have four hours into it at a rate of $40 an hour for a total of $120. Add the cost of materials to this. If a brochure takes two hours of your time at $40 an hour, the fee should be $80 plus materials.

Robert Brenner of Brenner Information Group says the median shop rate for desktop publishing services is $42 an hour.

Desktop publishers estimate and price a job by the time required, the number of pages, the complexity of the design, the characters typeset, or other factors. How you quote your job depends somewhat on the type of desktop publishing you specialize in. If you primarily produce newsletters, you will probably base your pricing on a standard page and add for nonstandard services, such as larger illustrations, special designs or typefaces.

Now that you know how to calculate pricing, here's a shortcut—buy Robert Brenner's *Pricing Guide for Desktop Publishing Services* (Brenner Information Group, 9282 Samantha Court, San Diego CA 92129; 619-538-0093). Not only does Brenner's loose-leaf book explain the concept of pricing and selecting a pricing strategy, it includes pricing tables by region (Figure 5.1) and a project cost estimating form (Figure 5.2, pp. 96-97). It offers specific pricing recommendations on file conversion, text creation, editing, imaging, design services, printer output, and more. The book costs less than two hours of your shop rate and will save you many, many hours at the calculator. Most important, it can make you both competitive and profitable. It even includes a shareware program for IBM compatibles to help you estimate and quote work on your computer.

CHANGES & ALTERATIONS (Typeface or Font Change)				
$/per	Survey %	Average	Typical	Maximum
Each	3.3%	6.43	5.00	25.00
Line	0.1%	0.70	0.70	1.00
Hour	61.7%	41.28	35.00	150.00
Job	2.0%	16.72	10.00	75.00
Minimum	1.2%	13.68	15.00	20.00

CHANGES - UPDATE PREVIOUS WORK (No Affect On Layout)				
$/per	Survey %	Average	Typical	Maximum
Each	2.9%	6.85	3.50	25.00
Line	0.1%	1.00	1.00	1.00
Hour	63.3%	42.60	40.00	150.00
Job	1.1%	22.40	10.00	75.00
Minimum	3.2%	16.83	15.00	50.00

CHANGES - UPDATE PREVIOUS WORK (Causes New Layout)				
$/per	Survey %	Average	Typical	Maximum
Each	2.4%	7.86	5.00	25.00
Line	0.1%	1.00	1.00	1.00
Hour	61.5%	40.88	35.00	150.00
Job	1.6%	17.71	10.00	75.00
Minimum	3.2%	10.52	15.00	50.00

CONSULTING				
$/per	Survey %	Average	Typical	Maximum
Hour	36.3%	49.50	45.00	1.50
Cost Plus %	0.4%	15.00	15.00	15.00

NOTE: Survey responses listed as $/minute, or $/day were converted to $/hr.

COORDINATING				
$/per	Survey %	Average	Typical	Maximum
Hour	8.9%	46.68	40.00	125.00
Cost Plus %	0.9%	15.00	15.00	20.00

DATABASE PUBLISHING				
$/per	Survey %	Average	Typical	Maximum
Hour	3.3%	39.60	35.00	75.00

DESKTOP VIDEO PRODUCTION				
$/per	Survey %	Average	Typical	Maximum
Hour	3.1%	70.45	50.00	300.00

Figure 5.1: A pricing guide can make the task of pricing your desktop publishing services easier (Courtesy of Brenner Information Group).

PROJECT COST ESTIMATING FORM

PROJECT: _____ DATE: _____
CLIENT: _____

Indirect Costs	Hours	x $/hour	=	Total/Task
Proposal preparation				
Client kickoff meeting				
Follow-up meeting 1				
Follow-up meeting 2				
Draft submission meeting				
Final submission meeting				
Telephone calls with client				
Travel time				
Close-out project				

Creative Costs	Hours	x $/hour	=	Total/Task
Conceptual development				
Style template				
Manuscript preparation				
Writing copy				
Designing charts				
Designing graphs				
Designing tables				
Designing illustrations				

Production Costs	Qty	x $/per ea	=	Total/Task
Disk file conversion				
Manuscript download				
Spelling/Grammar checking				
Prepare/Format text				
Import text into layout program				
Typography				
Place graphics				
Layout document				
First draft				
Corrections/Alterations				
Paste-up				
Final proof				

Figure 5.2: Page 1 of a typical Project Cost Estimating Form (Courtesy of Brenner Information Group).

Out-of-Pocket Expenses	Total
File conversion support (___ files @$___ ea)	
Laser proofs (___ @ $___ ea)	
Typeset output (___ @ $___ ea)	
Photographs (___ @ $___ ea)	
Illustrations (___ @ $___ ea)	
Stats (___ @ $___ ea)	
Color processing (___ @ $___ ea)	
Paste-up support	
Printing (___ cys @ $___ ea)	
Collating (___ shts @ $___ ea)	
Binding (___ pgs @ $___ ea)	
Travel (___ trips @ $___ ea)	
Delivery (___ trips @ $___ ea)	
Other	
Total Indirect Costs:	
Total Creative Costs:	
Total Production Costs:	
Total Out-of-Pocket Expenses:	
Shop Overhead Costs:	
TOTAL PROJECT COST:	

Figure 5.2, continued: Page 2 of a typical Project Cost Estimating Form (Courtesy of Brenner Information Group).

Selling the Value of Your Services

Now you know what your time costs you, what your competitors charge for their time and skills, as well as what customers expect to pay for your time and skills. So which figure is right? All and none. What you want is a price that will drive away about 10 percent of your prospects as too high, and another 10 percent as too low.

Here's a technique that will make your business more profitable, put your business above your competitors, and keep your customers happy—sell value not price. How can a fancy restaurant charge five times as much as the diner next door for the exact same ingredients? They sell value. Call it ambiance or image or snobbery or nonprice considerations or whatever. The fancy restaurant makes the client's purchase an event rather than just a transaction. The fancy restaurant treats the client like a person rather than a number, gives extra service, uses fine dinnerware, and decorates the food to look more appetizing.

You'll see the same technique—selling value rather than price—in any competitive business where one firm wants to stand out above the others. Chevys are sold on price, Cadillacs are sold on value—and both are built by General Motors. Value dictates that, whether the price is large or small, you will get your money's worth.

So how does a desktop publisher sell value? By offering services that other desktop publishing service do not, by using high-quality papers and production equipment, or by simply turning questions of price into discussions of value.

You can offer many extra services that don't cost much to implement yet add value to your service. Some desktop publishing services offer free seminars on how small businesses can design their own documents. The cost to your desktop publishing service is minimal, but it establishes you as an expert in desktop publishing and gives you an opportunity to reach people who do their own document design.

Value-priced desktop publishing services can step ahead of their competition by providing services the clients might normally perform themselves, such as addressing and mailing brochures at no additional charge above postage. Such a service gives the desktop publisher another chance to sell his value to the client or prospect. The work can be done by a responsible young person or by yourself as you watch evening TV.

Imagine seeing a can of tomato sauce on the grocer's shelf that is discolored, dented, the label torn. You'd probably pass it by for one that looked neat, fresh, and undamaged. Yet the contents of each can may be of exactly the same quality. Appearance does make a difference—especially in the desktop publishing business. For just a few dollars more, your business can develop a clean, professional appearance that will tell prospects and customers that you offer quality. Keep your office neat and orderly. Dress professionally. Use quality papers.

Price is the cost of something; Value is its worth. Why is your service worth something?

- You're knowledgeable; you know about desktop publishing and how to produce a valuable product.
- You're efficient; you know how to work smart to get the job done in less time.
- You're honest; you will not knowingly mislead your client or charge for services not performed.
- You're helpful; you want to solve the client's problem, not just perform a job.
- You're fair; you charge a reasonable fee for an important service.
- You're accessible; you respond to questions, you answer telephone calls, you follow up with clients.

Successful desktop publishing services don't shun the question of pricing or apologize for high rates. They look forward to the question, so that they can explain why their service is worth more than that of other desktop publishers. They sell—and give—value.

Managing Desktop Publishing Tasks

By breaking down the job into specific tasks and scheduling each one, you can ensure that all tasks are completed on time.

You can also prioritize your jobs into most important, less important, and least important to make sure that you're always doing what's most valuable to your business. A most important job is one with the shortest deadline, the quickest payout, the most important customer, the greatest opportunity for your desktop publishing firm.

Of course, this doesn't mean that any of your customers are less important than any other. All have equal potential for helping your business succeed either through jobs they hire you to complete or through other customers they refer to you. But the cash customer who must have a proposal published for a 2 P.M. sales meeting has a greater need for your services than does the customer who needs you to produce business cards sometime this month. So you prioritize your work based on the customer's need as well as your own.

Successful desktop publishing services reduce costs through scheduling to balance both the customer's need and their own, by:

- Keeping accurate time records by project (Figure 5.3)
- Grouping similar jobs together during the same time period, such as design work, style sheet modification, and printing
- Giving highest priority to jobs that provide the business with the greatest cash flow

A monthly planner can help with long-term planning and help you develop your daily planner or list of things to do. There are many other organizational tools that can help in your business.

Managing Time

How can the desktop publishing service business owner ensure that his or her time is well managed? First, by organiz-

DESKTOP PUBLISHER'S TIME SHEET

ABC DESKTOP PUBLISHING SERVICES

OPERATOR: _____

PROJECT	START TIME	END TIME	TOTAL TIME	ACTIVITY

Figure 5.3: Sample desktop publisher's time sheet.

ing work space so that important papers don't get lost and unimportant papers do. You can also make a rule that you will avoid handling papers more than once. If you pick up a piece paper, make a decision regarding it right then if possible.

Set up a regular work schedule. It may be from 7 A.M. to 6 P.M. or 8 A.M. to 5 P.M. or 6 A.M. to 6 P.M. Whatever it is, try to stick to it. And, if you manage your time well, you will be able to. If you have one time of the day that seems more productive for you than others, plan your most important functions around it.

What about travel and waiting time? Take work with you in a briefcase or purchase a laptop computer that you can use to keep productive every minute. As your time management skills improve, you'll learn how to do more than one thing at a time. You could be making job notes or talking with a key employee or gathering information on an upcoming project while you're waiting to talk with a client.

Meetings seem to be one of the biggest time-wasters there are. But you can change this by organizing all of your meetings. To be productive, meetings must have a purpose or agenda and a time limit. Even if you didn't call the meeting, if you see that it has no focus or structure you can step in and say, "I have another appointment in an hour. What topics do we have to cover in that hour?" then list those topics as the agenda.

One more time management tip—use one of the popular time-management planning systems to help you get the most out of your day. They include Day Timer (Day Timers, Inc., One Day-Timer Plaza, Allentown PA 18195-1551; 800-225-5005), Day Runner (Harper House, Inc.) and Planner Pad (Planner Pads, Inc., 5088 S. 107th St., Omaha NE 68127; 402-592-0666). These and other systems give you a place to record appointments, daily to-do lists, special projects and their steps, as well as a contact book for names and addresses. If you spend most of your time in the office at a computer, there are numerous contact management and scheduling pro-

Time and stress are closely related. The lack of time to do what you need to do often increases personal stress. How do you manage both? Here are some ideas from successful desktop publishers:

- Plan your time and establish priorities on a daily to-do list.
- Decide what your prime time is and do your most important or difficult tasks then.
- Set business hours, specific times when you're at work and times when you turn on the answering machine because you're on duty but off call. You, your customers, and your family will appreciate knowing your set routine, even though you know that for special events or emergencies you can break that schedule.
- Confirm all of your appointments one-half day before the appointment—afternoon for next morning or morning for that afternoon. It'll save you time, and your clients will appreciate the consideration.
- If you're working from your home, give your business as much of a separate and distinct identity as possible. Although you might save a few dollars by using the dining room table as a desk and a cardboard box as a file cabinet, the stress and strain of operating without proper space and supplies will take its toll.
- Have a separate room or area for your business, with a separate entrance if clients visit. Consider soundproofing, so your family won't be bothered by your noise and vice versa. In addition to the psychological and physical comfort of having a separate room for your home office, the IRS requires it in order for you to make a legitimate claim for tax deductions.

grams that will help you manage your time. If you use a portable computer, you can install these programs on it and carry this information wherever you go.

Hiring Good Employees

The best way to hire the right person for the job is to clearly define what skills are needed to perform it. Once you know what it takes to do the job, you can match the applicant's skills and experience to the job's requirements. This step will probably come easy for you if you're hiring a desktop publisher, but office help or other support functions will require more thought.

Once you have a job description on paper, decide what skills the person must have to fill the job. Then, estimate the value of this service to your business. Finally, determine how much other employers in your area are paying for these skills.

When you know the kinds of skills you need in your new employee, you're ready to contact sources that can help you recruit job applicants.

Each state has an employment service (Department of Employment, Unemployment Bureau, or Employment Security Agency). All are affiliated with the United States Employment Service and local offices are ready to help businesses with their hiring problems. The state employment service will screen applicants for you by giving aptitude tests if any are available for the skills you need. Passing scores indicate the applicant's ability to learn the work. So, be as specific as you can about the skills you want.

Private employment agencies will also help in recruitment. However, the employee or the employer must pay a fee to the private agency for its services. This fee can be from a month's to as much as a year's salary.

Another source of applicants is a Help Wanted sign in your own office window. Of course, a lot of unqualified applicants may inquire about the job, and you cannot simultaneously interview an applicant and talk on the phone to a customer.

Newspaper advertisements are another source of applicants. You reach a large group of job seekers, and if you used a blind box address, you can screen them at your convenience. If you list an office phone number, you may end up on the phone with an applicant instead of a customer.

Job applicants are readily available from local schools. The local high school may have a distributive or cooperative education department where the students work in your office part time while taking trade or business courses at school. Many part-time students continue with their employer after they finish school. Consider local and regional business schools as well. The students are often more mature and more motivated to work than high school students.

You may also find job applicants by contacting friends, neighbors, customers, suppliers, current employees, local associations, service clubs, or even a nearby armed forces base. However, don't overlook the problems of such recruiting. What happens to the goodwill of these sources if they recommend a friend whom you do not hire; or if you have to fire the person they recommend?

Your choice of recruitment method depends on what type of person you're looking for, your location, and your method of managing your business. You have many sources available to you. A combination may serve your best needs. The important thing is to find the right applicant with the correct skills for the job you want to fill, whatever the source.

Understanding and Paying Taxes

Like it or not, the government is your business partner. And, as your partner, it receives a portion of your profits—even before you do. However, government can also help you make a profit through the Small Business Administration,

Department of Commerce, state corporate divisions, and numerous other business services.

The owner-manager of a small business plays two roles in managing taxes. In one role, you're a debtor. In the other, an agent or tax collector, whether you want to be or not.

As a debtor, you're liable for various taxes, and you pay them as part of your business obligations. For example, each year you owe federal income taxes, which you pay out of the earnings of your business. Other tax debts include state income taxes and real estate taxes. You may also pay inventory and equipment or personal property taxes on your business assets.

As an agent, you collect various taxes and pass the funds on to the appropriate government agency. If you have employees, you deduct federal income, social security insurance or FICA taxes and, in some states, you collect state income taxes from the wages of your employees. If your state or city requires sales tax on your desktop publishing services, you will collect it from your customers and pass it along to the government.

If you are a proprietor, you pay your income tax as any other individual citizen. Your income, expenses, and profit or loss are calculated on Schedule C, which is filed with your annual Form 1040. A partnership files its own tax forms and passes the profits on to the partners for filing on their personal income tax forms. A corporation files on IRS Form 1120 or short form 1120A. Sub-Chapter S corporations file on IRS Form 1120S. Self-employment tax—social security insurance for the self-employed—is reported on your IRS 1040 form using Schedule SE.

Individual proprietors and partners are required by law to put the federal income tax and self-employment tax liability on a pay-as-you-go basis. That is, you file a Declaration of Estimated Tax (Form 1040 ES) on or before April 15, then make payments on April 15, June 15, September 15, and January 15.

Income tax returns from a corporation are due on the 15th of the third month following the end of its taxable year, which may or may not coincide with the calendar year. To find out more about your tax obligations, contact your regional IRS office (or call 1-800-829-3676) for the following publications.

IRS Publications

- *Tax Guide for Small Business* (Publication 334)
- *Guide to Free Tax Services* (Publication 910)
- *Your Federal Income Tax* (Publication 17)
- *Employer's Tax Guide* (Circular E)
- *Taxpayers Starting a Business* (Publication 583)
- *Self-Employment Tax* (Publication 533)
- *Retirement Plans for the Self-Employed* (Publication 560)
- *Tax Withholding and Estimated Tax* (Publication 505)
- *Business Use of Your Home* (Publication 587)

In addition, there are a number of federal forms you'll need for good record keeping and accurate taxation:

- Application for Employer Identification Number (Form SS-4), if you have employees
- Tax Calendars (Publication 509)
- Employer's Annual Unemployment Tax Return (Form 940)
- Employer's Quarterly Federal Tax Return (Form 941)
- Employee's Withholding Allowance Certificate (W-4) for each employee

- Employer's Wage and Tax Statement (W-2) for each employee
- Reconciliation/Transmittal of Income and Tax Statements (W-3)
- Instructions for Forms 1120 and 1120A for corporate taxes

Action Guidelines

As you can see, there are many responsibilities to managing the day-to-day operation of your desktop publishing service. They include controlling operating costs, keeping helpful records, producing quality documents at fair prices, managing employees, and paying required taxes. Here are some things you can do today to apply what you've learned in this important chapter.

- ✔ Estimate your desktop publishing service's operating costs.
- ✔ Develop an estimated operating budget for your desktop publishing service, including sales, costs, and profit.
- ✔ Design or select a simple record-keeping system, including journals and ledgers or accounting software.
- ✔ If you plan to have employees, establish a payroll system.
- ✔ Set up equipment records and keep them off-site.
- ✔ Establish your business's hourly rate and develop your price list.
- ✔ List ways you can sell value over price.
- ✔ Develop your own process for producing effective documents.
- ✔ Establish a simple but usable time management system.
- ✔ Call the IRS toll-free number to order appropriate booklets and forms.

Chapter 6

MARKETING YOUR DESKTOP PUBLISHING SERVICE

Who will buy desktop publishing services from you? What is your business's market? A market is simply the group of prospects who would most benefit from your services. The market for your desktop publishing service is made up of those who potentially could benefit from your service. That's a very broad definition that will apply to you and to your competitors. Defining your desktop publishing service's market means determining the characteristics of those who would most benefit from your unique combination of knowledge, skills, and resources.

This chapter will help you define your market and efficiently reach it.

Understanding Marketing

The first step to defining your market is to define who you are to them. Because there are dozens of types of desktop publishers—and hundreds of potential markets—we will use broad examples. But you'll quickly get the idea and be able to apply it to your specialty.

For example, how would you define the market for your short-document desktop publishing service when you can only work evenings and weekends and cannot use your home for an office? A prospect for this service is someone who is currently working and cannot take time off work to come to an office. In fact, your not having a regular office can be turned into a marketing advantage, as you offer the convenience of meeting customers in their home for the interview. You work together designing the document on paper or a laptop computer, then do the actual production at home or another site. By defining your unique benefits, you can best define your prospects or market.

Let's say that the best opportunity for you and your skills is to specialize in producing business stationery for businesses that have recently moved or plan to move in the near future. Your prospects are those who currently own a business and are considering relocation within your market. So how do you find these prospects? First, you go where they go. You read the business section of area newspapers for announcements, you make contacts within moving companies that specialize in moving businesses, and you work with the display advertising department of newspapers. You can also advertise in the newspaper's business section, offering your desktop publishing services.

One desktop publisher determined that there wasn't enough of a market for desktop publishing in her small community, so she decided to market exclusively to businesses in a nearby metropolitan area. She established a process where she would fax drafts back and forth at low cost then produce the final documents and ship overnight. Because her overhead and wages were less than those of desktop publishers in the metro area, she was able to competitively price her services and gain extensive business.

To market her service, she advertised in a metro business magazine, stressing her lower, "country" rates and including her toll-free telephone and fax numbers. She then developed a one-page newsletter with tips on effective document design and mailed or faxed it to anyone who called her. She built her credentials as well as used technology to expand her market.

Obviously, how you approach your prospects as a desktop publishing service will be somewhat different. Yet the principles will be the same. You will first determine whether there is sufficient opportunity for you to build your business and whether potential competitors are already adequately serving a market. Then you will focus your attention and your marketing on those who can best use your services.

Your prospects are those who have been influenced by your advertising or recommended by satisfied customers. They are former customers, newcomers to the area, customers who need immediate help, and your competitors' dissatisfied customers. They are people who have never before required desktop publishing services, as well as those who are looking for a new document supplier.

Some start-up desktop publishing service begin their business by serving customers who their current or former employer cannot serve. By taking these customers, services reduce the amount of marketing to develop customers. Most start-up desktop publishing services then pay a marketing fee or a finders fee to these business sources. It's another reason to maintain a good relationship with all of your past and current employers.

Let's look at marketing even closer, with specifics on how to develop a profitable market for your desktop publishing service.

How to Market Your Desktop Publishing Services

Marketing is a science. It's not a perfect science, where the answer to a question is always the same. It's a science based on data, information, knowledge, and wisdom. Data is easy to obtain and build into usable information. From this information comes knowledge and, eventually, wisdom. Wisdom is what makes your business profitable. Marketing builds your business.

The purpose of marketing is to get more customers. That's it. If you're new to business, the purpose is to get your first customers. If you've established a substantial business, the purpose is to keep your customers.

There are dozens of ways that you can market your services to prospects and customers. They include the many forms of advertising, as well as literature, direct mail, and telephone marketing.

Understanding Your Customers

Customers are vital to your business. That's obvious. The better quality of customers, the greater the success of your business.

Who needs the services of a desktop publisher? Prospects for desktop publishing services include small businesses, shopping centers, marketing managers, writers, professional offices, service businesses, and many others.

There are two ways of defining prospective customers or prospects—demographics and psychographics.

Demographics is a study of statistics about people—where they live, how much they make, how they buy, their favorite brands. Retailers use census information to build demographics that help them in deciding where to build a store. Desktop publishing services can use demographics, too. They can learn who would use their services and, then, where to find them.

As an example, a desktop publisher specializing in producing employee newsletters must know more than the fact that a prospect manages employee relations at an area business. The desktop publisher must also understand employee relations and how newsletters benefit businesses. This information is available through human resources books and periodicals as well as through business communications associations.

Psychographics is the study of why people buy. You would think that most people buy for logical reasons. However, even in the business world, people often buy for emotional reasons and justify their decision with logical reasons. Knowing why your clients buy will help you sell to them more effectively.

If you've built a solid reputation in your area as a desktop publisher whose name means quality, you can sell that name. People want to go with a winner, so you will get some jobs just because people know your reputation. So learn what makes your customers buy and help them to buy from you.

Understanding your customers is so important that large corporations spend millions of dollars annually on market research. Although some formal research is important, a small business can usually avoid this expense. Typically, the owner or manager of a small desktop publishing service knows the prospective customers personally. From this foundation, understanding your customers can be built by a systematic effort.

Understanding buyers starts with the realization that they purchase benefits rather than products or services. Consumers don't select toothpaste. Instead, some will pay for decay prevention. Some seek pleasant taste. Others want bright teeth, or perhaps any toothpaste at a bargain price will do.

Similarly, industrial purchasing agents are not really interested in drills. They want holes. They insist on quality appropriate for their purposes, reliable delivery, safe operation, and reasonable prices. Video games are fun. Cars are visible evidence of a person's wealth, lifestyle, or self-perceptions.

You must find out, from their point of view, what customers are buying—and why. Understanding your customers enables you to profit by providing what buyers seek—satisfaction.

So, people don't buy documents. They purchase positive impressions on their customers. They want to develop an image of consistent quality that will make what they sell seem more valuable to their prospects. They want speedy and accurate service. They could care less about buying a document! Put yourself in their shoes and determine what they want, why they buy, when they buy, and how and where they buy these benefits. Then you will understand how to reach them.

Finding Prospects

A prospect is a prospective customer, someone who could potentially use your service but hasn't done so yet. They may not have heard of your service, or they may not know enough about your service to determine its value, or they simply haven't been asked.

Who is a prospect for your desktop publishing service? Of course, that depends on what service you perform for customers. If you're a desktop publisher who specializes in publishing booklets for health clinics, these are your prospects. To turn these prospects into customers, you must first think as they think, only faster. As an example, a clinic may determine—or you may point it out to them—that they are losing the valuable time of staff who must stop to answer customer questions about the clinic. A booklet describing the clinic, its procedures, its hours, and its billing practices will help the clinic's clients and save the staff from having to explain it. If this is your market, make sure that medical clinics and professional offices in your area know of your service. These are your prospects.

The U.S. Census Bureau is an excellent source of statistical data for market research. Based on the every decade's census, the Bureau divides large cities into census tracts of about 5,000 residents within Standard Metropolitan Statistical Areas (SMSAs). Data on these tracts cover income, housing, and related information that can be valuable to you. Results of the 1990 census are now available. For this and other market information, contact the Office of Business Liaison, U.S. Department of Commerce, Washington DC 20230. The Bureau of the Census offers business statistics, data, and special demographic studies among its services.

How should you keep track of your prospects? There are many ways, depending on how many there are and how you plan to market to them. Some desktop publishing service owners use 3 x 5 inch file cards available at any stationery store. A typical prospect card will include both basic information—name, owner, address, telephone number, business, etc.—as well as qualifying information and notes from prospecting contacts.

There are also contact management software programs that will help you keep track of prospects. They range in price from about $50 for a simple system to $500 or more for a specialized prospecting system that can even help you write personalized sales letters. As an example, a good contact management program will give you standard fields for the firm name, contact name(s), address, telephone and fax numbers, the names of mutual friends or associations, and information about contacts. Some even serve as a simple order entry form. If you're making regular telephone calls to prospects, the program may help you schedule call-backs, maintain records of conversations, and write personalized proposals that can be quickly printed for mailing or even faxed to your prospect while they're still thinking about you.

Selling Desktop Publishing Services

The majority of your prospects will make first contact with you by telephone. They may have read your ad in the newspaper or phone book, or heard about you from a mutual acquaintance. In any case, it is vital that you make the most of this first contact to answer their questions while getting answers to your own questions about them.

The prospects want to know:

- Why they should use your service?
- Are you qualified to produce an effective document?
- Are your services worth the price?
- Are you trustworthy?

You want to know:

- What's your name and how can I contact you?
- How did you hear about my service?
- What do you need to know to make a decision to hire me?

Establishing an Advertising Program

The purpose of advertising is to tell your potential customers why they will benefit from using your services. The best way to do so is to let your other customers tell your prospects how much they gain from your service. That's called word-of-mouth advertising, and it is the most valuable type of advertising there is. Unfortunately, it is also the slowest to develop. Your first satisfied client may, in conversations, mention your good service once or twice a month. After hearing that a number of times and when they are looking for your service, that prospect may call you for your service. By that time, you may be out of business due to lack of work.

Desktop publishing services must advertise. How much should you spend on advertising? Successful desktop publishing services typically spend about 5 percent of their estimated annual sales on advertising. This can be as low as 3 percent or

A typical telephone script would be:

Thanks for calling A-B-C Desktop Publishing Service. My name is John Smith. Your name? Yes, <u>name</u>, how can I help you today?

Give the caller a chance to respond and to identify the purpose of the inquiry. To sell you must first listen.

I appreciate your call, <u>name</u>. I'm certain that you're calling to find the most efficient way of producing effective documents that reach your clients. We can help. In fact, we've designed and produced over _____ documents for businesses just like yours. And we make it easy. Would you like to know more?

A prospect will ask how you develop a document, ask about price, or want to know if you have experience in their specific field. Before you answer, ask:

That's a good question, <u>name</u>. First, let me ask a couple of questions. What type of marketing problems does your business face? How did you hear about A-B-C Desktop Publishing Service? What factors do you feel are most important in selecting a desktop publishing service?

Listen carefully and take notes. Then answer their questions as appropriate, assuring them that you are professional, reliable, and cost-effective. Depending on what desktop publishing services you sell, you may want to quote a price over the telephone or hold off until you have a face-to-face meeting.

Learn all that you can from the prospect. It not only develops a bond, it also displays that you are a good listener—an important characteristic for success. In addition, you'll learn more about your market and what they are looking for in a desktop publishing service.

as high as 7 percent. Services located in areas where competition is tough may spend as much as 10 percent on advertising. For example, a desktop publishing service with estimated annual sales of $100,000 should spend between $3,000 and $7,000 a year on advertising and promotion—or $10,000 or more in a competitive market.

Successful desktop publishing service owners suggest that the majority of an advertising budget should be spent during months when business is typically slower. Rather than an ad budget of $250 a month, slow months may require a budget of $400 or more, while busy months will have a budget of $100. Long-term advertising, such as the phone book's Yellow Pages, require monthly payments.

Advertising is based on impressions. Every time your prospect sees or hears your name, you make an impression. It may be something small like seeing the sign in front of your

---

AAA Desktop Publishing Service

- Complete Graphics and Typographic Services
- Page Layout and Design
- Newsletters
- Brochures
- Flyers
- Business Plans
- Menus
- Complete PostScript Scanning, Proofing, and 2,400-DPI Laser Imaging
- MD-DOS, Windows, and Macintosh compatibility

123 Main Street, Yourtown, USA 12345   555-1234

Sample Yellow Pages ad for a desktop publishing service

business or an ad in the local paper. Or it may be a listing in the Yellow Pages or a positive (or negative) comment made by an acquaintance.

Each impression is cumulative. After numerous impressions, large and small, your prospect may bring your name into the "possible source" part of his or her brain. Then, when a legitimate need for your service arises, the prospect considers you as a supplier. Think about it. How many times did you see or hear about Honda or Mr. Coffee before you even considered trying them. Probably dozens or even hundreds of impressions were made. Remember that negative feelings about these products are also impressions.

The point is that you will need to positively impress your prospects many times and in many ways before they can be upgraded to a customer.

Besides advertising, there are numerous ways you can make positive impressions on prospects. Desktop publishers can speak to local groups on a variety of business topics. Kiwanis, Rotary, Lions, and other service organizations are always looking for informative—and free—speakers. Just remember that it must be informative, not just an opportunity to sell. Make sure you have an effective brochure or fact sheet that you can give to people who want to know more about your service.

Many successful desktop publishing services develop much of their business through referrals. That is, they sell their services to those who work with people looking for business documents—printers, copy shops, publishers, technical training services, etc.

Of course, you can enhance word-of-mouth advertising by developing testimonials. When you have a client who expresses satisfaction with your service, ask the client to write a testimonial letter. The letter, on business stationery, will describe how professional your service is and how well you respond to the needs of customers.

Unfortunately, only a small percentage of those who say they will write a testimonial letter will actually do so. The problem isn't sincerity, it's time. Most customers just don't have the time to write such a letter. So some desktop publishers offer to write a draft of the letter themselves—or hire a freelance writer to do so—and send it to the customer for approval and typing on their letterhead. A well-written testimonial from a respected businessperson will be worth literally thousands of dollars in new business to you. You can copy it and include it in with your brochure, quote from it in advertisements, and pass it out to prospects. It will be your best form of advertising.

To encourage satisfied customers and their testimonials, some desktop publishing services establish and promote a policy of satisfaction guaranteed. The profits lost are usually replaced by the profits gained through this policy. It is a helpful persuasion tool when trying to close a sale.

Of course, make sure that you have a customer's written permission to use any testimonials you quote in advertising.

Free Advertising and Publicity

There are many effective ways to advertise or publicize your desktop publishing service at little or no cost. Exactly which methods you use depend somewhat on your specialization.

If you're personable and comfortable doing it, offer to host a radio call-in show on business topics. Or you can become a regular guest on someone else's talk show. The publicity will make you a local celebrity as well as an authority on business documents and publishing.

Once you have your business card printed, carry a stack with you wherever you go. Pass them out to anyone who may be or may know a prospect. As you stop for lunch, put your business card on the restaurant's bulletin board. Put your card on the bulletin board at the local market. All it costs is the

```
News Release                    March 12, 1995
For Immediate Release,
For more information call
Jane Smith at 555-1234
```

New Business Offers
Economical Publishing Services

Jane Smith, experienced graphic artist, recently opened a new business in the downtown mall, offering publishing services to area businesses and individuals.

Ms. Smith says AAA Desktop Publishing Services "offers complete design and typesetting services at reasonable costs." She notes that by using computers her firm is able to reduce production time and costs.

"Smaller businesses just can't afford traditional typesetting services," she says. "Our service puts professional and powerful documents within the reach of everyone."

Ms. Smith, a native of Yourtown, has worked as a graphic designer for three local businesses, managing a variety of publication projects.

"I saw a need for cost-effective publishing services in this area," said Smith. "We can quickly publish newsletters, brochures, flyers, business plans, and a variety of other documents. We can also produce documents from computer files developed by our clients."

AAA Desktop Publishing Services is located at 123 Main Street, next to Sterling Business Services. Their hours are 8-6, M-F and 10-2, Sat. The telephone number is 555-1234.

-30-

Sample news release, announcing the opening of your desktop publishing service.

News Release   March 12, 1995
For Immediate Release,
(Sample brochure attached)
For more information
call Jane Smith at 555-1234

Local Business Wins National Award

AAA Desktop Publishing Services recently won an award for the "Best Brochure Design" sponsored by the National Association of Desktop Publishers.

Owner Jane Smith says the brochure "was quite a challenge and a really fun project for us." The brochure was for ABC Garbage Disposal, a local business. The company asked for a unique design that would help it enhance the image of its business and inform customers of newly added recycling services.

"It was quite a success," says ABC Garbage Disposal Service owner Frank Ernest. "Our business has increased by 30 percent since we mailed our brochure out three months ago. We're very pleased with AAA Desktop Publishing Services' design."

Ms. Smith, a native of Yourtown, has worked as a graphic designer for three local businesses, managing a variety of publication projects. She started AAA Desktop Publishing Services six months ago in the downtown mall. She has been a member of the National Association of Desktop Publishing Services for four years.

"This is my third design award and I'm very please with the honor," says Smith.

AAA Desktop Publishing Services is located at 123 Main Street, next to Sterling Business Services. Their hours are 8-6, M-F and 10-2, Sat. The telephone number is 555-1234.

Sample publicity/news release on noteworthy event that can be used to publicize your desktop publishing service.

price of a business card. In fact, order separate business cards for your specialties, such as business documents, employment documents, and promotion packages.

Many desktop publishing service overlook one of the best sources of free advertising: publicity. As you start your business, write a short article or press release and give copies to your local newspaper, radio stations, shoppers, and other media. Include information about your business, such as owners, experience, affiliations, background, expertise, purpose of the business, location, market, and contact information. If your market is across an industry rather than a geographic area, send this press release to magazines for the trade. You can also promote your business and get "free" advertising by offering to write a weekly newspaper column on local business in exchange for an ad in the paper.

Also consider establishing an award or scholarship at a local high school, trade school, or community college in your business's name. You can use the award to promote your business in the local media and will be able to deduct the cost as a legitimate business expense.

One more proven idea—seek awards. Join professional and business associations and enter all applicable business contests. If you win, whether first place or honorable mention, use the award as an opportunity to promote your business through local and national media.

Using Newspaper Advertising

Most homes in the U.S. and Canada receive a newspaper. From the advertiser's point of view, newspaper advertising is convenient because, if necessary, production changes can be made quickly and you can often insert a new advertisement on short notice, depending on the frequency of the publication. Another advantage is the large variety of ad sizes newspapers offer. The disadvantages of newspaper advertising include the cost of producing a large ad that will stand out among other large ads, the short throw-away life of a newspaper, and the poor printing quality of newspapers. If you do select to advertise in newspapers, establish a consistent schedule, rather than a hit-and-miss advertising program. Most important, ensure that the program is realistically within your budget.

Most desktop publishing services advertise in the business section of the local newspaper. Depending on the size of the community, the frequency of the paper, and the cost, an ad in the Business Services Directory can be a valuable investment. Find out where your competitors are advertising and develop a better ad. You may want to use a name like ABC Desktop Publishing Service to ensure that your ad is listed first or prominently include a feature or benefit that your competitors don't offer—"Satisfaction Guaranteed," "24-Hour Turnaround," "Specializing in Marketing Campaigns and Collateral."

If there is sufficient cost advantage, sign a contract for a specific number of column inches of advertising for the year rather than a standard size. By doing so you are earning a discount as well as allowing for business fluctuations. Reduce the size of your ad when business is good and increase it when you need more business. Some contracts will allow you to change your ad as much as once a week while still earning a substantial discount.

Using Yellow Pages Advertising

Many desktop publishers say that an ad in the Yellow Pages is one of their best sources of new business. In most locations, if you purchase a business telephone line you will get a listing in one category of your local Yellow Pages. In some areas this is optional.

The listing may be as simple as:

> AAA Desktop Publishing Service, 123 Main St. 555-1234

Or the firm name can be in capital letters such as:

> **AAA DESKTOP PUBLISHING SERVICE**
> 123 Main St. 555-1234

Or you can include information on your specialty and even an alternate telephone number such as:

> AAA Desktop Publishing Service
> Specializing in Brochures and Ads
> 123 Main St... 555-1234
> If no answer. 555-2345

Many businesses upgrade their listings with space ads. A space ad is simply an advertisement that takes up more space than a line or two and is usually surrounded by a box.

To determine the size and cost of an appropriate space ad, check your local and nearby telephone book's Yellow Pages under headings for Desktop Publishing, Typesetting, and related topics. Look for your competitors. When a potential client looks in the Yellow Pages, which ads stand out the best? Which have the greatest eye-appeal? Which are easiest to read? Remember that you don't need the largest ad in the phone book, you need the one that is most cost-effective for you.

The last few pages in your Yellow Pages frequently has information on how to select a space ad. You'll see terms like *double half, double quarter, and triple quarter,* as well as *columns.* It's actually quite easy to follow. Most larger telephone books have four vertical columns per page; community phone books in rural areas are half-size with only two columns per page. So a triple quarter is three columns wide and a quarter-page long; a double half is two columns wide and a half-page long.

There will often be a toll-free telephone number for ordering a space ad or listing. You may also find the number in the front of the phone book under Business Telephone Service or a similar title. Ask about cost and availability of color in your ad. The firm that produces your telephone book will help you design and write your ad. Then they will supply a layout of the ad and a contract for you to sign. Most Yellow Pages listing or space ad contracts are for one year and can be paid in monthly installments with your phone bill.

How to Build Repeat Business

A repeat customer is simply one who hires you for more than one job. If the customer is satisfied and needs your services again, you have a good chance of getting a repeat customer. You didn't have to go out and spend additional money on advertising or work extra hours to promote your business. Your quality of business promotes itself.

The best way to get repeat business is to ask for it. As you call up your clients to determine their satisfaction, also ask them:

- Do you have any other document jobs coming up?
- Would you like us to bid on them?
- What services do you expect to need from us in the coming year?
- Are there any related services that we could implement for you in the future?

You can also build repeat business by continually marketing your services to them. It is more productive to get more business from current customers than to find new ones. Here's how some successful desktop publishing service build repeat business:

- Send all customers a monthly newsletter with new information on how other businesses effectively use documents and a listing of other services you offer.
- To add value, perform extra services that other local desktop publishing service don't do for their customers, such as furnishing professional designs at a fraction of the cost of a designer.

How to Earn Referral Business

Earning referrals is one of the most powerful types of business promotion. A referral is simply when satisfied customers sell your services to prospective buyers. The word of a trusted businessperson is much more believable to prospects than is the word of an unknown businessperson or salesperson.

So how do you get your customers to refer prospects to you? You ask them. In fact, it should be an automatic question: Is there anyone whom you know who may also need our services? Ask it right after you close a sale, as you start a job, as you complete a job, and—especially—whenever anyone compliments an aspect of your work. Like this:

> *"I really appreciate the direct mail piece you designed for me. I'm sure it contributed to our 7 percent response rate."*
>
> *"I'm glad to hear that. Is there anyone whom you know who may also need our services?"*

In addition, once customers have referred others to you, many feel a stronger obligation to continue to use your services. Referrals not only help you grow your business, but also help you keep your current customers.

Action Guidelines

Learning how to effectively market your desktop publishing service can quickly separate you from your competition. There have been many proven marketing ideas offered in this chapter. To implement some of these idea for your desktop publishing, take the following actions:

✔ Define your desktop publishing service's market. Who are your prospects? Who needs and will buy your service?

✔ Start a database of prospective customers or referral sources—printers, publishers, etc.

✔ How and why do your prospective customers buy desktop publishing services? What are their expectations?

✔ Learn what your prospects have in common with each other. Do they read a specific newspaper or meet at a certain location?

✔ Write your own version of a telephone sales script.

✔ Establish a low-cost advertising campaign for reaching your prospective customers.

✔ Find customers who will write testimonial letters for you or allow you to write them on their behalf.

✔ Carry a stack of your business cards wherever you go and post them wherever you can.

✔ Develop a cost-effective Yellow Pages ad in conjunction with your telephone company's advertising department.

✔ Establish your own techniques for developing repeat and referral business as suggested in this chapter.

THE FINANCIAL SIDE OF YOUR DESKTOP PUBLISHING SERVICE

Business success is measured, in part, by financial success. In most cases, you will be monetarily rewarded in relation to the service you provide to others. The more you help, the more you earn. How much of that you keep depends on how well you manage your money.

The purpose of this chapter is to ensure that you gain and keep an appropriate amount of money for what you do. The chapter covers profits, cash flow, credit, financing, and other money topics.

Profit is simply the amount of money you have left over once you've paid all of your expenses. If you have more expenses than income, you have a loss. Pretty simple.

Of course, there's much more to profit and loss than numbers on paper. Your business can actually show a profit on paper, yet not have any cash. In fact, many profitable businesses go out of business each year because of negative cash flow.

How can you keep the cash flowing in your desktop publishing service business? By keeping good records, watching expenses, and tracking the flow of cash in and out of your business. Before we cover cash flow, let's see how successful desktop publishing services set up and use an efficient money-tracking system.

Managing Your Money

As the owner of a desktop publishing service, you need accurate information on a regular basis to ensure that your business is running smoothly. As a single-person firm you may have all the information you need in your head. But as your firm grows you will need some information daily, other information weekly, and still other data on a monthly basis. Let's take a look at what you will need and when.

You will want the following information on a daily basis:

- Cash on hand
- Bank balance
- Daily summary of sales and cash receipts
- Daily summary of monies paid out by cash or check
- Correction of any errors from previous reports

You can either prepare this information yourself, have an office employee prepare it for you, or rely on your accountant for monthly reports. While daily records will not show you trends, they will help you get a feel for the level of business that you're doing. And you'll be able to spot problems before they become serious.

You or someone in your employ should prepare a weekly report on your firm. While still not sufficient for long-term planning, weekly figures will help you make small corrections in the course your business is taking. Weekly, you'll want:

- Accounts receivable report listing accounts that require a call because they are more than 60 days overdue

- Accounts payable report listing what your business owes, to whom, and if a discount is offered for early payment
- Payroll report, including information on each employee, the number of hours worked during the week, rate of pay, total wages, deductions, net pay, and related information
- Taxes and reports required by city, state, and federal governments

Your weekly reports should be prepared by the end of business Friday so you can review them over the weekend or early Monday morning.

Once a month, you will want to review information that accumulated through your daily and weekly reports but was too small to analyze clearly. As monthly data, information about cash flow, accounts receivable, and other parts of your business make more sense—and can be more easily acted upon. Here are some of the reports and information you will want to see every month:

- Monthly summary of daily cash receipts and deposits
- General ledger including all journal entries
- Income statement showing income for the prior month, expenses incurred in obtaining the income, overhead, and the profit or loss
- Balance sheet showing the assets, liabilities, and capital or current worth of the business
- Check reconciliation that shows what checks were deposited, which were applied by payees against your business checking account, and to verify the accuracy of the cash balance
- Petty cash fund report to ensure that paid-out slips plus cash equals the beginning petty cash balance

- Tax payment report showing that all federal tax deposits, withheld income, FICA taxes, state and other taxes have been paid
- Aged receivables report showing the age and balance of each account (30, 60, 90 days past due)
- Summary of Schedule C entries

Let's take a closer look at your most important monthly reports: income statement, balance sheet, and cash-flow forecast.

Income Statements

Your income statement is a detailed, month-by-month tally of the income from sales and the expenses incurred to generate the sales. It is a good assessment tool because it shows the effect of your decisions on profits. It is a good planning tool because you can estimate the impact of decisions on profit before you make them.

Your income statement includes four kinds of information:

1. Sales information lists the total revenues generated by the sale of your service to clients.

2. Direct expenses include the cost of labor and materials to perform your service.

3. Indirect expenses are your costs, even if your service is not sold, including salaries, rent, utilities, insurance, depreciation, office supplies, taxes, and professional fees.

4. Profit is shown as pretax income (important to the IRS) and after-tax or net income (important to you and your loan officer).

Balance Sheets

Your balance sheet is a summary of the status of your business—its assets, liabilities, and net worth—at an instant in time. By reviewing your balance sheet along with your income statement and your cash flow forecast, you will be able to make informed financial and business planning decisions.

The balance sheet is drawn up using the totals from individual accounts kept in your general ledger. It shows what you have left when you pay all your creditors. Remember, assets less liabilities equals capital or net worth. The assets and liabilities sections must balance—hence the name balance sheet. The balance sheet can be produced monthly, quarterly, semi-annually, or at the end of each calendar or fiscal year. If your record keeping is manual you will be less likely to develop a frequently update balance sheet. Many accounting software programs can give you a current balance sheet in just a couple of minutes.

While your accountant will be most helpful in drawing up your balance sheet, it is you who must understand it. Current assets are anything of value you own such as cash, inventory, or property that the business owner can convert into cash within a year. Examples of fixed assets are land and equipment. Liabilities are debts the business must pay. They may be current, such as amounts owed to suppliers or your accountant, or they may be long-term, such as a note owed to the bank. Capital, also called equity or net worth, is the excess of your assets and retained earnings over your liabilities.

Cash Flow Forecasts

Your business must have a healthy flow of working capital to survive. Cash flow is the amount of working capital available in your business at any given time. To keep tabs on cash flow, forecast the funds you expect to disburse and receive over a specific time. Then you can predict deficiencies or surplus in cash and decide how best to respond.

A cash-flow forecast serves one other very useful purpose in addition to planning. As the actual information becomes available, compare it to your monthly cash-flow projections to see how accurately you are estimating. As you do this, you will be giving yourself on-the-spot business training in making more accurate estimates and plans for the coming months. As your ability to estimate improves, your financial control of the business will increase.

Every time that you purchase on credit, you add interest costs to your business. If you had more cash, you would be able to save on interest expense. For this and other reasons, you can reduce your costs by increasing cash flow.

The cash-flow forecast identifies when cash is expected to be received, when it must be spent to pay bills, and how much will be needed. It also allows the owner to identify where the necessary cash will come from. For example, will the funds needed for the purchase of a new computer come from collecting accounts receivable or a loan?

The cash-flow forecast enables you to plan for shortfalls in cash resources so short-term working capital loans—or a line of credit—may be arranged in advance. Or, you will know when you have excess cash that could be invested in the business or elsewhere for higher return. It helps you schedule purchases and payments so you can borrow as little as possible. Because not all sales are cash sales, you must be able to forecast when accounts receivable will be cash in the bank, as well as when regular and seasonal expenses must be paid.

The cash-flow forecast may also be used as a budget, helping you increase your control of the business through comparing actual receipts and payments against forecasted amounts. This comparison helps you identify areas where you can manage your finances better.

A cash-flow forecast or budget can be prepared for any period of time. However, a one-year budget matching the fiscal year of your business is the most useful. Many successful desktop publishing services prepare their cash-flow forecasts on a monthly basis for the next year. It should be revised no less than quarterly to reflect actual performance in the previous three months of operations and to verify projections. Revising monthly is better.

All businesses, no matter how small or large, function on cash. Many businesses become insolvent because they don't have enough cash to meet their short-term obligations. Bills must be paid in cash, not potential profits. Sufficient cash is therefore one of the keys to maintaining a successful business. You must understand how cash moves or flows through the business and how planning can remove some of the uncertainties about future requirements.

Desktop publishing services face a continual cycle of events that may increase or decrease the cash balance. Cash is decreased in the acquisition of equipment or supplies. It is reduced in paying off the amounts owed to suppliers (accounts payable). Selling your services generates accounts receivable. When customers pay, accounts receivable is reduced and the cash account is increased. However, the cash flows are not necessarily related to the sales in that period, because customers may pay in the next period.

Desktop publishing services must continually be alert to changes in working capital accounts, the cause of these changes, and their implications for the financial health of the company.

The ability to forecast cash requirements is indeed a means of becoming a more efficient desktop publishing service owner/manager. The change in the cash can be readily determined if you know the net working capital and the changes in current liabilities and current assets other than cash.

Let:

NWC = net working capital
CA = change in current assets other than cash
CL = change in current liabilities
Cash = change in cash

Because net working capital is the difference between the change in current assets and current liabilities:

$$NWC = CA + Cash - CL$$
$$Cash = NWC - CA + CL$$

This relationship shows that if we know the net working capital (NWC), the change in current liabilities (CL), and the change in current assets other than cash (CA - cash), we can calculate the change in cash. The change in cash is then added to the beginning balance of cash to determine the ending balance.

At any given level of sales, it's easier to forecast the required accounts payable and receivables, than net working capital. To forecast this net working capital account, you must trace the sources and application of funds. Sources of funds increase working capital. Applications of funds decrease working capital. The difference between the sources and applications of funds is the net working capital.

The following calculation assumes that the balance sheet is indeed in balance. That is, the total assets equal total liabilities plus owner's equity.

$$\text{Current Assets} + \text{Noncurrent Assets} + \text{Retained Earnings} =$$
$$\text{Current Liabilities} + \text{Long-term Liabilities} + \text{Equity}$$

Rearranging this equation:

$$\text{Current Assets} - \text{Current Liabilities} = \text{Long-term Liabilities} +$$
$$\text{Equity} - \text{Noncurrent Assets} - \text{Retained Earnings}$$

Because the equation must balance and both sides represent net working capital, a change in any of these categories will affect net working capital. For example, if long-term liabilities and equity increase or noncurrent assets decrease, net working capital increases. This change would be a source of funds. If noncurrent assets increase or long-term liabilities and equity decrease, net working capital decreases. This change would be an application of funds.

Typical sources of funds contributing to net working capital are funds provided by operations, disposal of fixed assets, issuance of stock, and borrowing from a long-term source. The typical applications of funds subtracting from net working capital are purchase of fixed assets, payment of dividends, retirement of long-term liabilities, and repurchase of equity.

Improving Cash Flow

As you can see, to grow your desktop publishing service you need cash. Once you've analyzed cash flow and determined that you need more of it, what can you do? Depending on the specific type of business you own, you can find increased cash in your accounts receivable and in your inventory.

Accounts receivable represent the extension of credit to support sales. In your business, the types and terms of credit you grant are set by established competitive practices. As an investment, the accounts receivable should contribute to overall Return on Investment (ROI).

Excessive investment in accounts receivable can hurt ROI by tying up funds unnecessarily. One good way to judge the extent of accounts receivable is to compare your average collection period with that of rivals or the industry average. If your average collection period is much longer than your competitors' or the industry norm, your accounts receivable may be excessive.

If they are excessive, it may be that you're not keeping tight control of late payers. You can check this by developing an aging schedule. An aging schedule shows the distribution of accounts receivable and whether payment is on time or late.

Failure to closely monitor late payments ties up investment and weakens profits. The more overdue accounts become, the greater is the danger that they will be uncollectable and will have to be written off against profits.

If the aging schedule does not reveal excessive late accounts, your average collection period may be out of line simply because your credit policy is more liberal than most. If so, it should translate into more competitive sales and greater profits. Otherwise, you should rethink your credit program.

Building Your Business's Credit

Credit is simply someone else's faith that you will keep your promise to them. You buy a computer system on credit and the lender believes that you will repay what you've borrowed—or that assets you're offered as collateral can be sold to cover the amount of the loan. So how do you build credit? Easy. You borrow a small amount, pay it back; borrow a larger amount, pay it back, and so on.

A good way to start building your business credit is to use personal assets—signature, real estate equity—as collateral for your business. One enterprising desktop publishing service owner simply applied for a credit card in his business name from the same company that sponsored his long-standing personal credit card. He asked for a small credit limit, used it and paid it off, then asked for an increased credit limit. Meantime, he used the credit card as a reference for a new account with a supplier. Other new business people use equity in their homes or investment land as collateral for credit with banks and suppliers.

Getting a Loan

A recent survey of small businesses reported that 23 percent had lines of credit, 7 percent had financial leases, 14 percent had mortgage loans, 12 percent had equipment loans, and 25 percent had vehicle loans. For larger firms, the percentage is about double in each category.

The ability to get a loan when you need it is as necessary to the operation of your business as is the right equipment. Before a bank or any other lending agency will lend you money, the loan officer must feel satisfied with the answers to these five questions:

1. What sort of person are you, the prospective borrower? In most cases, the character of the borrower comes first. Next is your ability to manage your business.
2. What are you going to do with the money? The answer to this question will determine the type of loan and the duration.
3. When and how do you plan to pay it back? Your lender's judgment of your business ability and the type of loan will be a deciding factor in the answer to this question.
4. Is the cushion in the loan large enough? In other words, does the amount requested make suitable allowance for unexpected developments? The lender decides this question on the basis of your financial statement, which describes the condition of your business, and on the collateral pledged.
5. What's the outlook for business in general and for your business in particular?

When you set out to borrow money for your firm, it is important to know the kind of loan you need from a bank or other lending institution. Let's discuss loans and other types of credit. There are numerous types of loans available, all with unique names depending on the lender. Let's consider them.

Signature Loan. A signature loan holds nothing in collateral except your promise to pay the lender back on terms that you both agree upon. If your money needs are small, you only need the money for a short time, your credit rating is excellent, and you're willing to pay a premium interest rate because you're not using physical collateral, a signature or character loan is an easy way to borrow money in a hurry.

Credit Cards. Many a small business has gained at least some of its funding from the owner's personal credit card. Computers, printers, books, office supplies, office overhead, and other costs can be covered with your personal credit card. However, interest rates on credit cards are extremely high—sometimes double of what you might pay on a collateral loan. But they offer you quick cash when you need it. If this is an option, talk to your credit card representative about raising your credit limit. It will be much easier to do so while you're employed by someone else.

Line of Credit. A line of credit is similar to a loan, except that you don't borrow it all at once. You get a credit limit, say $50,000, which you can tap anytime you need money for business purposes. The most common form is the revolving line of credit that you can draw from when business is off and pay back when business is good, providing that you don't exceed your limit. A line of credit is an excellent way for a desktop publishing service to work through the ups and downs of seasonal business. With some restrictions, a line of credit can be established using a portion of your home equity as collateral. Using a secured equity earns you a lower interest rate.

Cosigner Loans. A cosigner loan should be one of the most popular loans for small businesses, but many business people never consider it. Simply, you find a cosigner or a co-maker with good credit or assets to guarantee your loan. If you have a potential investor who believes in your business but doesn't want to put up the cash you need, ask him or her to cosign for a loan with you. Your chances of receiving the loan are much better. Some cosigners will require that you pay them a fee of 1 to 4 percent of the balance or a flat fee; others will do it out of friendship or the hope of future business from you. In any case, consider cosigner loans an excellent source of capital for your new desktop publishing service.

Equipment Leasing. If you're purchasing equipment or other assets for your business, the supplier may loan or lease the equipment to you. This often requires about 25 percent down, so be ready to come up with some cash of your own.

Collateral Loan. A collateral loan is one in which some type of asset is put up as collateral; if you don't make payments, you will lose the asset. So the lender wants to make sure that the value of the asset exceeds the amount of the loan and will usually lend 50 to 75 percent of asset value. A new desktop publishing service owner often does not have sufficient collateral—real estate or equipment—to secure a collateral loan without using personal assets, such as a home.

Sometimes you can get a loan by assigning to the bank a savings account. In such cases, the bank holds your assignment and your passbook. If you assign an account from another bank, the lending bank asks the other bank to mark its records to show that the account is held as collateral.

Another kind of collateral is life insurance. Banks will lend up to the cash value of a life insurance policy. You have to assign the policy to the bank. If the policy is on the life of an executive of a small corporation, corporate resolutions must be made authorizing the assignment. Most insurance companies allow you to sign the policy back to the original beneficiary when the assignment to the bank ends. Some people like to use life insurance as collateral rather than borrow directly from insurance companies. One reason is that a bank loan is often more convenient and may carry a lower interest rate.

For more information on business credit, write to the Federal Trade Commission (Washington DC 20580; Attn: Public Reference) and ask for their free booklet on *Getting Business Credit.*

Managing Interest Rates

Money is a commodity, bought and sold by lenders. Just as with other products, you can often save money by shopping around. Here are some points to consider as you shop for money.

First, are there any loan fees or other charges required to set up or service the loan? Some lenders will require that a loan fee of 1 to 2 percent or more be paid in advance. Others will even roll the loan fee into the loan—so you actually pay interest on interest. Others will deduct a monthly service fee from each payment as it is made. This arrangement is not necessarily bad; after all, the lender must make a profit in some manner. Just make sure that you understand what the actual cost of the loan is before you agree to it. You also need to know actual interest rates as you compare rates between lenders.

Second, consider whether your best option is fixed rate or variable rate interest. For fixed rate loans the interest rate is the same throughout the life of the loan. Variable rate interest can vary during the term of the loan and is tied to changes in an outside factor or index, which is a measurement of the cost of the money to the lender. The rate can change only by predetermined increments, called caps, both annually and during the life of the loan. The difference between the lender's cost and your interest rate is called the spread. Covered in that spread are the lender's sales costs, office overhead, salaries, and profit. The amount of risk the lender is taking in making the loan also influences the spread. Higher risk means a larger spread. There are numerous indexes used to establish the cost of money. Review all of the options with your lender, ask which one makes the most sense for your needs, and get a second opinion.

Keep in mind that variable rate interest reduces the amount of risk the lender is taking, especially on long-term loans. The lender is virtually assured that, unless the money market goes crazy and goes over the cap, it will make its margin of profit on the loan. Lower risk means lower rates. The point is that you shouldn't disqualify variable rate loans from consideration. In many cases, they cost less than fixed rate loans and many lenders are more willing to make them.

To make sure that you get the best interest rate available, don't jump into the arms of the first loan offer that comes to you. Shop around and compare. You may eventually decide to take that first offer, but only because you've found nothing better.

But don't worry about getting the absolute lowest interest rate available. You may want to accept your regular lender's loan terms, even though it's a quarter of a percentage point higher, in order to maintain a mutually profitable relationship. That quarter point may only mean a few dollars and will reinforce your business relationship with your lender.

SBA Guaranteed Loans

The volume of business loans guaranteed by the SBA has increased from $3 billion in 1989 to approximately $7.5 billion in 1993. According to the SBA, the average loan was for $250,626 over a term of 11.5 years. About one-fifth of these loans went to companies that were less than two years old. Here is a summary of current SBA loan opportunities:

SBA 7(a) Guaranteed Loans. SBA 7(a) Guaranteed Loans are made by private lenders and can be guaranteed up to 80 percent by the SBA. Most SBA loans are made under this guaranty program. The maximum guaranty of loans exceeding $155,000 is 85 percent. SBA has no minimum size loan amount and can guarantee up to $750,000 of a private sector loan. SBA provides special inducements to lenders providing guaranteed loans of $50,000 or less. The lender must be a financial institution that "participates" with the SBA. The small business submits a loan application to the lender, who makes the initial review. If the lender cannot provide the loan outright, the lender may request an SBA guaranty. The lender then forwards the application and its analysis to the local SBA office. If the loan is approved by the SBA, the lender closes and disburses the funds.

SBA Direct Loans. Loans of up to $150,000 are available only to applicants unable to secure an SBA-guaranteed loan. Direct loan funds are available only to certain types of borrowers such as handicapped individuals, nonprofit sheltered workshops, Vietnam-era veterans, disabled veterans, businesses located in high-unemployment areas and owned by low-income individuals, or businesses located in low-income neighborhoods. The applicant must first seek financing from at least two banks in their area.

Microloans. SBA Microloans, the newest SBA loan opportunity, is intended for smaller businesses that only need a few thousand dollars. The typical SBA microloan is for about $10,000, though some lenders offer up to $25,000 for worthwhile small business ventures. Contact your regional SBA office for additional information and requirements, or call the Association for Enterprise Opportunity (415-495-2333).

Applications. If you're interested in applying for an SBA guaranteed or direct loan, call your local regional office of the Small Business Administration. Even better, ask for the names of SBA-certified lenders in your area. The SBA loan program, notorious for its paperwork requirements, can be expedited by a lender that knows how to work within the system. You'll get your loan faster. In fact, bankers who have "preferred-lender" status can handle your SBA loan without the SBA even being involved.

How to Offer Credit to Your Customers

Most successful desktop publishing services offer 30-day accounts to established clients but strictly enforce a no-credit policy for new clients. Some require all fees up front with the order. Others require a 50 percent deposit. Many offer payment by credit card.

Using credit card services such as Visa, MasterCard, American Express, and Discover can transfer bad debts problems to others and increase cash flow for your business. However, there is an initial setup cost and ongoing service charges. The credit card service will charge you a service charge of 2 to 5 percent on each transaction. Talk with your lender about accepting credit card payments from your customers.

How to Improve Financial Planning

Financial planning affects how and on what terms you will be able to attract the funding you need to establish, maintain, and expand your business. Financial planning determines the human and physical resources you will be able to acquire to operate your business. It will be a major factor in whether or not you will be able to make your hard work profitable.

The balance sheet and the income statement are essential to your business, but they are only the starting point for successful financial management. The next step is called ratio analysis. Ratio analysis enables you to spot trends in a business, comparing its performance and condition with the averages of similar businesses in the same industry. To do this, you should also compare your ratios with your previous performance over several years. Ratio analysis can be the most important early warning indicator for solving business problems while they are still manageable.

Members of trade associations often will share their balance sheet, income statement, and management ratios with other members through studies and reports published by the association. It's just one more good reason to join one of the local or national desktop publishing trade associations. These percentages can help you in determining whether you're operating your desktop publishing service as efficiently as other firms in the industry.

Important balance sheet ratios measure liquidity (a business's ability to pay its bills as they come due) and leverage (the business's dependence on creditors for funding).

Liquidity ratios indicate the ease of turning assets into cash and include the current ratio, quick ratio, and working capital.

Current Ratio. The current ratio is one of the best known measurements of financial strength. It is calculated as follows:

$$\text{Current Ratio} = \frac{\text{Total Current Assets}}{\text{Total Current Liabilities}}$$

The main question this ratio answers is: Does your business have enough current assets to meet the payment schedule of its current debts with a margin of safety? A generally acceptable current ratio is 2 to 1. That is, twice as many current assets as current liabilities.

Let's say that you—or your lender—decide that your current ratio is too low. What can you do about it?

- Pay some debts.
- Combine some of your short-term debts into a long-term debt.

- Convert fixed assets into current assets.
- Leave in earnings or put profits back into the business.
- Increase your current assets with new equity (bring some more cash into the business).

Quick Ratio. The quick ratio is sometimes called the acid test ratio and is one of the best measurements of liquidity. It is calculated as follows:

$$\text{Quick Ratio} = \frac{\text{Cash + Securities + Receivables}}{\text{Total Current Liabilities}}$$

The quick ratio is a much more exacting measure than the current ratio. By excluding inventories (typically small in desktop publishing services), it concentrates on the truly liquid assets with fairly certain value. The quick ratio helps answer the question: If all sales revenues should disappear, could my business meet its current obligations with the readily convertible, "quick" funds in hand?

A ratio of 1:1 is considered satisfactory unless the majority of your quick assets are in accounts receivable, and the pattern of collection lags behind the schedule for paying current liabilities.

Working Capital. Working capital as discussed earlier, is more a measure of cash flow than a ratio. The result of the following calculation must be a positive number:

Working Capital = Total Current Assets - Total Current Liabilities

Lenders look at net working capital over time to determine a company's ability to weather financial crises. Bank loans are often tied to minimum working capital requirements. The ideal ratio of gross revenue to working capital is 10:1.

A general rule about these three liquidity ratios—current ratio, quick ratio, and working capital—is the higher the better, especially if your business is relying heavily on creditor money or financed assets.

Leverage Ratio. The leverage or debt/worth ratio indicates the business's reliance on debt financing (loans), rather than owner's equity. It is calculated as follows:

$$\text{Leverage Ratio} = \frac{\text{Total Liabilities}}{\text{Net Worth}}$$

Generally, the higher this ratio the more risky lending you money will be considered. The ideal ratio is 1:1.

Net Profit Margin. The net profit margin ratio is a percentage of sales dollars left after subtracting the cost of goods sold and all expenses except income taxes. It provides a good opportunity to compare your company's return on sales with the performance of others in the industry. It is calculated before income tax because tax rates and tax liabilities vary from company to company. The net profit margin ratio is as follows:

$$\text{Net Profit Margin Ratio} = \frac{\text{Net Profit Before Tax}}{\text{Net Sales}}$$

Action Guidelines

Money is obviously vital to the success—and future—of your desktop publishing service. Here are some proven ways you can make sure that your business stays in business:

- ✔ Establish a simple system for keeping informed on the financial status of your business on a regular basis.
- ✔ Watch your balance sheet carefully and learn to apply ratios to ensure success.
- ✔ Keep a running cash flow forecast, no matter how simple, to ensure that money will continue to come in when you need it.
- ✔ Learn how to develop and use your net working capital, rather than borrowing from the bank.
- ✔ Keep your relationship with your banker open and friendly—just in case.
- ✔ Talk to your banker about becoming a credit card merchant.

SUCCEEDING AS A DESKTOP PUBLISHING SERVICE

R aising a child goes well beyond the birthing process and getting him or her into kindergarten. Success will take many years of both enjoyment and problem-solving. The same is true of your desktop publishing service. This final chapter offers a collection of ideas and techniques from successful desktop publishing service owners and other business people on how to make your business grow. It tells you how to solve small problems before they become big ones, manage employees and temporary help, insure against potential losses for your business and your employees, manage risks and catastrophes, and keep an eye on the future.

How to Solve Common Business Problems

As the owner of your own desktop publishing business you deal with problems on a daily basis. So learning how to effectively solve problems can dramatically affect the growth and success of your business. Most business owners solve problems by intuition. By learning the skill of problem solving—just as you would learn the skill of document design—you will become more comfortable with solving problems and reduce the inherent stress of your job.

A problem is any situation that presents an obstacle to your desire to move ahead. Here are a few examples:

- A computer program doesn't function as it should.
- A part you need for your copy machine is unavailable.
- An employee is undermining your authority with clients.
- New business income is down.
- A customer is complaining about errors in a document.
- You're two payments behind, and a leasing company is threatening to repossess your computer.

Problems arise from every facet of human and mechanical functions, as well as from nature. Some problems we cause ourselves, such as hiring an untrainable employee. Other problems are caused by forces beyond our control, such as a flood or tornado. Problems are a natural, everyday occurrence of life. However, if mismanaged, they cause tension and frustration that only makes matters worse. We must learn how to deal with problems in a logical, rational fashion.

The solutions to some problems, such as how to plan next week's particularly heavy work schedule, are typically simple and will require only a few moments of contemplation and planning. However, some problems, such as how to increase income by $100,000 in the next six months, are more critical to your operation and will require more time and effort. In fact, for critical problems, you may want to set aside a full day for analyzing the problem and finding the best solutions.

Recognizing a Problem. You must first recognize that a problem exists before you can solve it. Here is where your approach to problem solving is crucial. You should not allow the problem to intimidate you. Don't take it personally. Approach it rationally and remind yourself that every problem is solvable if it is tackled appropriately.

Fear of failure can block your ability to think clearly. You can overcome this natural fear if you:

- follow a workable procedure for finding solutions.
- accept the fact that you can't foresee everything.
- assume that the solution you select is your best option at the time.
- accept the possibility that things may change and your solution fail.

Defining the Problem. Once you recognize that a problem exists, your next step is to identify or define the problem itself. You can do so by asking yourself such questions as:

- What exactly happened?
- What started the problem?
- Did something unexpected occur?
- Did something break?
- Were there unexpected results?

Then ask questions that help you identify the nature of the problem:

- Is this a person, equipment, or operational problem?
- What product or service does it involve?
- Is the problem tangible or intangible?
- Is the problem internal or external to the firm?

How important is this problem to the scheme of things? Ask yourself:

- Is this problem disrupting operations?
- Is this problem hampering sales?

- Is this problem causing conflict among people?
- Is this problem affecting personnel and their productivity?
- Is this problem affecting business goals and, if so, which ones?
- Is this problem affecting customers, suppliers, subcontractors, or any other external people?

Some problems are "100-year floods" that don't occur often enough to warrant extensive attention. Ask these questions:

- Is it a problem that occurred in the past and the main concern is to make certain that it doesn't occur again?
- Is it a problem that currently exists and the main concern is to clear up the situation?
- Is it a problem which might occur in the future and the basic concern is planning and taking action before the problem arises?

The answers to these questions will help you focus on the true problem. You can't effectively research the causes of a problem until you have a clear definition of what the problem is. Sometimes, managers spend many hours on what they perceive as the problem only to learn, after seeking the causes, that something else was really the problem.

Selecting the Best Solution

Using the questions above as a guide, develop a list of possible solutions. Go through this list and cross out those that obviously won't work. These ideas aren't wasted, for they impact on those ideas that remain. In other words, the best ideas you select may be revised using ideas that won't work.

Break the remaining solution down into its positive effects and negative effects. To do this, some business owners write each solution they are considering on a separate piece of paper.

Below the solution, they draw a vertical line down the center of the sheet, labeling one column Advantages and the other column Disadvantages. Finally, they analyze each facet of the solution and its effect on the problem, listing all the advantages and disadvantages they can think of.

One way to come up with advantages and disadvantages is to role-play each solution. Call in a few of your employees, friends, or relatives and play out each solution. Ask them for their reactions. Based on what you observe and their feedback, you will have a better idea of the advantages and disadvantages of each solution you're considering.

After you complete this process for each primary solution, select those solutions that have the most significant advantages. At this point, you should be considering only two or three. In order to select the most appropriate solution from these, consider:

- Cost-effectiveness
- Time constraints
- Availability of manpower and materials
- Your own intuition

Before you actually implement the chosen solution, you should further evaluate it. Ask yourself:

- Are the objectives of the solution sound, clear, and simple?
- Will the solution achieve the objectives?
- What are the possibilities that it will fail and in what way?
- How can I reduce the possibility of failure?

Taking Action

Finding the solution doesn't mean that the problem is solved. Now you need to design a plan of action to implement the

> When designing the plan of action, consider:
>
> - Who will be involved in the solution?
> - How will they participate?
> - Who will be affected by the solution?
> - How will they be affected?
> - What course of action will be taken?
> - How should this course of action be presented to employees, customers, suppliers, and others?
> - When will the action start and be completed?
> - Where will this action happen?
> - How will this action happen?
> - What's needed to make it happen?

solution properly. Designing and implementing the plan of action is equally as important as finding the solution. The best solution can fail without good execution.

Design a plan of action chart, including all the details needed to implement the plan and when each phase should happen. Keep in mind, though, that the best plans have setbacks for any number of reasons. A key person may be out for illness or a supplier may ship materials late or a change at the customer's site may require that the timetable be changed.

As each phase of your plan of action is implemented, you should ask yourself whether your goals were achieved, how well they were achieved, and did it work smoothly. To check your own perceptions of the results, get as much feedback as possible from your customers and employees. What you may think is working may not be considered to be by those closer to the action. Always remember that customers and employees are your most valuable resources in successfully carrying out your solution.

How to Profitably Manage Employees

The majority of employees in the labor force are under a merit-increase pay system, though their pay increases generally result from other factors. This system requires periodic review and appraisal of employees' performance.

An effective employee appraisal plan improves two-way communications between the manager and the employee. It also relates pay to work performance and results, while helping employees improve by understanding job responsibilities and expectations. An employee appraisal plan also provides a standardized approach to evaluating job performance.

Such a performance review helps not only the employee but also the manager, who can gain insight into the organization. An open exchange between employee and manager can show the manager where improvements in equipment, procedures, or other factors might improve employee performance. Try to foster a climate in which employees can discuss progress and problems informally at any time throughout the year.

Use a standardized written form for appraisals. An appraisal form should cover the results achieved, quality of performance, volume of work, effectiveness in working with others in the firm and with customers and suppliers, initiative, job knowledge, and dependability.

To keep your pay administration plan in tune with the times, you should review it at least annually. Make adjustments where necessary and don't forget to retrain supervisory personnel. This isn't the kind of plan that can be set up and then forgotten.

During your annual review, ask yourself if the plan is working for you. That's the most important question. Are you getting the kind of employees you want or are you just making do? What's the employee turnover rate? Do employees seem to care about the business? Most importantly does your pay administration plan help you achieve the objectives of your business?

Employee Benefits

Employee benefits play an important role in the lives of employees and their families, and they have a significant financial impact on your business. Desktop publishing services cannot be competitive employers if they don't develop a comprehensive benefit program. However, if not carefully managed, an employee benefit program can quickly eat up a small firm's profits.

A comprehensive employee-benefits program can be broken down into four components: legally required benefits, health and welfare benefits, retirement benefits, and perquisites (or perks).

Legally required benefit plans are mandated by law and the systems necessary to administer such plans are well established. These plans include social security insurance (FICA), workers' compensation insurance, and unemployment compensation insurance (FUTA).

Health and welfare benefits and retirement benefits can be viewed as benefits provided to workers in conjunction with statutory benefits to protect employees from financial hazards related to illness, disability, death, and retirement. Health and welfare plans are perhaps the most visible of all the benefit program components. They include medical care, dental care, vision care, short-term disability, long-term disability, life insurance, accidental death and dismemberment insurance, dependent care, and legal assistance.

Retirement plans help ensure that employees are able to maintain their accustomed standard of living upon retirement. Retirement-benefit plans basically fall into two categories: *defined contribution plans*, which provide employees with an account balance at retirement, and *defined benefit plans*, which provide employees with a projected amount of income at retirement.

Perquisite benefits, called perks, are any additional benefits, such as a company automobile or truck, professional association or club membership, paid tuition, extra vacation, personal expense account, credit cards, or financial counseling services.

Understanding Health and Welfare Plans

When purchasing a health and welfare plan, select a professional whose clientele is made up primarily of small businesses. In fact, if you can find one in your area, select one that's used and recommended by other desktop publishers. Your insurer needs to be aware of the special problems that face small businesses, especially in your trade. Generous plans that look attractive and logical today may become a financial burden . Remember that it is much easier to add benefits than it is to take them away.

Medical plans are usually the greatest concern of employers and employees. There are essentially two kinds of traditional medical plans. Major medical plans cover 100 percent of hospital and inpatient surgical expense as well as a percentage (typically 80 percent) of all other covered expenses. Comprehensive medical plans cover a percentage (again, generally 80 percent) of all medical expenses.

In both types of plans, the employee is usually required to pay part of the premium, particularly for dependents, as well as a deductible. Deductibles often range from $100 to $200 for single coverage and from $200 to $1000 per person for family coverage.

A comprehensive medical plan is typically less expensive because more of the cost is shifted to the employee. Any plan you design should include features for containing costs.

As an alternative to a traditional medical plan, an employer may contract with a Health Maintenance Organization (HMO) to provide employees with medical services. The main difference between a traditional medical plan and an HMO is that the traditional plan allows employees to choose their medical providers, while HMOs usually provide medical services at specified clinics or through "preferred" doctors and hospitals. HMOs trade flexibility for lower costs, which are often passed on to the employee through lower deductibles and premiums.

Disability insurance is an important but often overlooked benefit in small businesses. Disability insurance can support a principal in the event that he or she cannot continue working.

Group life insurance is a benefit employees have come to expect in many regions and trades. Such insurance is usually a multiple of an employee's salary. Be aware that the amount of insurance over a legally specified level is subject to taxation as income to the employee.

Recent legislation requires that employers who maintain medical and dental plans must provide certain employees the opportunity to continue coverage if they otherwise become ineligible through employment termination or other causes. In addition, new rules state that if a firm's health and welfare plan discriminates in favor of key employees, the benefits to those employees are taxable as income. Talk to your plan administrator about current laws and requirements.

Understanding Retirement Benefit Plans

Retirement benefit plans are either *qualified* or *unqualified* plans. A plan is qualified if it has met certain standards mandated by law. It is beneficial to maintain a qualified retirement plan because contributions are currently deductible, earnings on plan assets are tax-deferred, benefits earned are not considered taxable income until received, and certain distributions are eligible for special tax treatment.

Of the various qualified plans, profit-sharing plans, 401(k) plans, and defined benefit plans are the most popular.

A profit-sharing plan is a defined contribution plan in which the sponsoring employer has agreed to contribute a discretionary or set amount to the plan. Any contributions made to the participant's plan account are generally prorated based on compensation. The sponsoring employer makes no promise as to the dollar amount a participant will receive at retirement. The focus in a profit-sharing plan, and in defined contribution plans in general, is on the contribution. What a participant receives at retirement is a direct function of the contributions made to the plan and the earnings on such contributions during the participant's employment with the plan sponsor. At retirement, profit-sharing plan participants receive an amount equal to the balance in their account. Profit-sharing plans are favored by employers because employers can retain discretion in determining the amount of the contribution made to the plan.

Another type of defined contribution is the 401(k) plan. In a 401(k) plan, participants agree to defer a portion of their pretax salary as a contribution to the plan. In addition, the sponsoring employer may decide to match all or a portion of the participant's contributions. The employer may even decide to make a profit sharing contribution to the plan. Again, the focus is on the contribution to the plan. At retirement, participants will receive an amount equal to their account balance. Special nondiscrimination tests apply to 401(k) plans, which may reduce the amount of deferrals highly compensated employees are allowed to make and which somewhat complicate plan administration. The 401(k) plans are popular because employees can save for retirement with pretax dollars and employers can set up programs relatively inexpensively.

In direct contrast to a defined contribution plan, a defined benefit plan promises participants a benefit specified by a formula in the plan. The focus of a defined benefit plan is the retirement benefit provided instead of the contribution made. Plan sponsors must contribute to the actuarially determined amounts necessary to meet the dollar amounts promised to participants. Generally, benefits begin at retirement and are paid over the remainder of the employee's life, so a defined benefit plan guarantees a certain flow of income at retirement.

As a business owner, you can establish your own retirement plan, called a Self-Employed Pension (SEP) plan. Call the IRS for the booklet *Retirement Plans for the Self-Employed* (Publication 560).

How to Select the Best Plan

Designing and implementing an employee-benefit program can be a complicated process. Many small businesses contract with employee-benefit consulting firms, insurance companies, specialized attorneys, or accounting firms to assist in this task. As you establish your program, whether with a professional or not, ask yourself:

- What should the program accomplish in the long run?
- What's the maximum amount the business can afford to spend on a program?
- Am I capable and knowledgeable enough to administer the program?
- What kind of program will best fit the needs of employees?
- Should I involve employees in the design and selection of the benefit program? If so, how much and at what stage?

Certain retirement plans are more suitable for desktop publishing services than others, depending on your financial situation and the demographics of your employee group. Employers who are not confident of their future income may not want to start a defined benefit plan, which will require a specific level of contributions. However, if the employees are fairly young, a profit-sharing plan or 401(k) plan can be a more significant and appreciated benefit than a defined benefit plan. The 401(k) plans are very popular now that restrictions have limited IRAs. However, the nondiscrimination tests make it more difficult for small businesses to maintain 401(k) plans. If your work force is composed mainly of older employees, a defined benefit plan will be more beneficial to them, but more expensive for you to maintain.

Remember that while a qualified plan has many positive aspects, the qualified retirement plan area is complicated and well monitored by the government. Make sure you have adequate counsel before you decide on the most appropriate plan for your business.

How to Hire Temporary Help

How does your desktop publishing business cope with unexpected personnel shortages? Many businesses are facing this question whether the cause is seasonal peaking, several employees on sick leave, or an unexpected increase in business. For some tasks, many desktop publishing services use subcontractors. But for office work, a growing number hire help through temporary personnel services. In fact, many new desktop publishing services will start their business with part-time temporary office personnel instead of hiring full-time employees.

Using a Temporary Personnel Service

Temporary personnel services, listed in your Yellow Pages under Employment Contractors—Temporary Help, are not an employment agencies. Rather, they hire people as their own employees and assign them to companies requesting assistance. When you use a service, you're not hiring an employee; you're buying the use of the employee's time. The temporary personnel firm is responsible for payroll, bookkeeping, tax deductions, workers' compensation insurance, fringe benefits, and all other similar costs connected with the employee. You're relieved of the burden of recruiting, interviewing, screening, and basic skill training.

Most national temporary personnel companies also offer performance guarantees and fidelity bonding at no added cost to their clients. As important, you're relieved of the need for government forms and for reporting withholding tax, social security insurance, and unemployment compensation insurance.

If you need temporary personnel for a period of six months or more, it's usually more cost-effective to hire a full-time employee. Also, if the task requires skills or training beyond basic office skills, it may cost you less to pay overtime to an employee with those skills.

Using Temps Effectively

The key to successful use of temporary employees is in planning what type of help you will need, how much, and when. The better the information you give to the temporary service firm the more efficient they will be in supplying the correct person.

Before your temporary employee arrives on the job, there are a few things you should do. First, if possible, appoint one of your permanent employees to supervise the temporary employee and check on the progress of the work. Be sure this supervisor understands the job and its responsibilities. Next, let the rest of your permanent staff know that you're taking on extra help and that it will be temporary. Explain why the extra help is needed, and ask them to cooperate with the new employee in any way possible.

Have everything ready before the temporary employee arrives. The work should be organized and laid out so that the employee can begin producing with a minimum of time spent in adjusting to the job and the surrounding. Also, don't set up schedules that are impossible to complete within the time you allot. Try to stay within the time limits you gave the temporary help service but plan to extend the time period if necessary, rather than hurry the employee.

Finally, furnish detailed instructions. Describe your type of business and the services you offer. Help the temp feel comfortable and part of your team. Most temporary employees have broad business experience and can easily adapt to your requirements—if they know what they are.

The Risks of Business

You've learned how to increase sales and reduce expenses for your desktop publishing business. But even as your business grows and profits, you can still lose money. How?

- An employee is injured on the job and sues you.
- An employee runs off with money from your business.
- A fire or flood wipes out your office, equipment, and important records.
- A partner in your business files bankruptcy, and the courts attach your business.
- The local economy goes sour, and you can't find enough work for six months or more.
- A business partner is involved in a divorce settlement, and business assets must be sold to meet a court order.
- The IRS comes after you for a large tax bill you allegedly owe, taking over your bank account until everything is resolved.

The list goes on. There are many ways that an otherwise profitable business can quickly be thrown into a situation where its future is in jeopardy. What can you do about it? First, you can make sure you understand the risks involved in your business. And second, you can take precautions to ensure that the risks are minimal. They will never go away, but through smart risk management you can minimize them and prepare for the worst.

Identifying Potential Risks

Of course, the best time to minimize the risk of business disasters is before they happen. And the first step is identifying potential risks. Business risks that desktop publishing services typically face are:

- Acts of nature (fire, flood)
- Acts of man (theft, vandalism, vehicle accidents)
- Personal injury (employee or customer)
- Legal problems (suits, unfair trade practices, torts)
- Financial (loss of income, funding, or assets)
- Taxation (judgments, tax liens)
- Management (loss of partner or owner's capacity to manage)

Of course, every method of reducing risk—attorneys, insurance, binding agreements, security systems, fire alarms, etc.—costs money. So when is it more cost-effective to accept the risk rather than pay for products or services that eliminate it? It's a simple question with a simple answer—it all depends.

There are a number of ways that you can minimize your losses. They include preventing or limiting exposure to loss, risk retention, transferring risk, and insurance.

One principle of loss prevention and control is the same in business as it is in your personal life—avoid activities that are too hazardous. For example, don't leave cash or valuable equipment where it can be easily stolen.

A desktop publishing service owner may decide that the firm can afford to absorb some losses, either because the frequency and probability of loss are low or because the dollar value of loss is manageable. Maybe your desktop publishing business owns an older vehicle and your drivers have excellent safety records; so you decide to drop the collision insurance on this vehicle but retain it on a newer vehicle.

Insuring against Risks

The most common method of transferring risk is purchasing insurance. By insuring your business and equipment, you have transferred much of the risk of loss to the insurance company. You pay a relatively small amount in premium rather than run the risk of a much larger financial loss.

Of course, you can be overinsured or pay more than is necessary for the amount of risk that you transfer. That's why it's so important to select a reputable and professional insurance agent for your desktop publishing business, as discussed earlier. However, only you can decide which exposures you absolutely must insure against. Some decisions are already made for you: insurance required by law or by those with whom you do business. Workers' compensation insurance is an example of insurance that's required by law. And your bank probably won't lend you money for equipment, real estate, or other assets unless you insure them against loss.

Today, very few businesses—and especially desktop publishing services—have sufficient financial reserves to protect themselves against the hundreds of property and liability exposures that they face. What those exposures are, what their dollar value is, and how much is enough, are difficult questions. That's why, as you build a team of business professionals to help you effectively manage your business, you should choose an insurance professional.

Four kinds of insurance are essential to your business—fire, liability, automobile, and workers' compensation insurance. Selecting from among the dozens of available policies and

Business Insurance Tips

Fire Insurance

- You can add other perils—such as windstorm, hail, smoke, explosion, vandalism, and malicious mischief—to your basic fire insurance at a relatively small additional fee.
- If you need comprehensive coverage, your best buy may be one of the all-risk contracts—such as the $1 million umbrella policy—that offer the broadest available protection for the money.
- Remember that the insurance company may compensate your losses by paying actual cash value of the property at the time of the loss; it may repair or replace the property with material of like kind and quality; or it may take all the property at the agreed or appraised value and reimburse you for your loss.
- Even if you have several policies on your property, you can still collect only the amount of your actual cash loss. All the insurers share the payment proportionately.
- Special protection other than the standard fire insurance policy is needed to cover the loss by fire of accounts, bills, currency, deeds, evidence of debt, and securities.
- After a loss, you must use all reasonable means to protect the property from further loss or run the risk of having your coverage canceled.
- In most cases, to recover your loss you must furnish within 60 days a complete inventory of the damaged, destroyed, and undamaged property showing in detail quantities, costs, actual cash value, and amount of loss claimed.
- If you and your insurer disagree on the amount of the loss, the question may be resolved through special appraisal procedures provided for in the fire insurance policy.
- You may cancel your policy without notice at any time and get part of the premium returned. The insurance company also may cancel at any time within a specified period, usually five days, with a written notice to you.

Liability Insurance

- You may be legally liable for damages even in cases where you used "reasonable care."
- Under certain conditions, your business may be subject to damage claims, even from trespassers.
- Most liability policies require you to notify the insurer immediately after an incident that might cause a future claim. This holds true no matter how unimportant the incident may seem at the time it happens.

- Even if the suit against you is false or fraudulent, the liability insurer pays court costs, legal fees, and interest on judgments, in addition to the liability judgments themselves.
- You can be liable for the acts of others under contracts they have signed with you, such as subcontractors. This liability is insurable.

Automobile or Vehicle Insurance
- When an employee uses a car on your behalf, you can be legally liable even though you don't own the car or truck.
- You can often get deductibles of almost any amount—$250, $500, $1,000—thereby reducing your premiums.
- Automobile medical-payments insurance pays for medical claims, including your own, arising from vehicular accidents regardless of the question of negligence.
- In most states, you must carry liability insurance or be prepared to provide a surety bond or other proof of financial responsibility when you're involved in an accident.
- You can purchase uninsured motorist protection to cover your own bodily injury claims from someone who has no insurance.
- Personal property stored in a car or truck and not attached to it is not covered under an automobile policy.

Workers' Compensation Insurance
- Federal laws require that an employer provide employees a safe place to work, hire competent fellow employees, provide safe tools, and warn employees of existing danger. Whether or not an employer provides these things, they are liable for damage suits brought by an employee and possible fines or prosecution.
- State law determines the level or type of benefits payable under workers' compensation insurance policies.
- Not all employees are covered by workers' compensation insurance laws. The exceptions are determined by state law and therefore vary from state to state.
- You can save money on workers' compensation insurance by seeing that your employees are properly classified. Rates for workers' compensation insurance vary from 0.1 percent of the payroll for "safe" occupations to about 25 percent or more of the payroll for very hazardous occupations.
- Most employers can reduce their workers' compensation insurance premium cost by reducing their accident rates below the average. They do this by using safety and loss-prevention measures established by the individual state.

options can be somewhat confusing to most business people. However, the following information will guide you in making the right decisions for the right reasons.

How to Survive Business Cycles

No businesses are truly recession-proof. All businesses have cycles where sales become easier or harder to make. Desktop publishing services are subject to the same business cycles that most businesses face. Even so, there are steps you can take to minimize the impact of the market's downswing and extend the benefits of its upswing.

First, determine the business cycle for your market. Reviewing income and financial records from prior years, or checking with the local chamber of commerce, you can draw a chart illustrating the local business cycle. In your region, it may be that most of the market for your service occurs in the spring and summer. Or maybe in the winter and fall. Or the cycle may be fairly equal across the year, but alternate years may fluctuate up or down. The first step to coping with recessions in the local business cycle is to determine exactly what and when that cycle is.

The next step is to begin planning for it. That is, if you're coming up to a typically slower period, determine what you need to do. In past years, how much has income dropped? For how long? Can you find income sources in other specialties where the cycle moving is up? What expenses can you reduce? Do you have an employee who would like a seasonal layoff to catch up on other interests?

Maybe you need to dramatically reduce your expenses and debts for this period. If so, list them out now, determine which will naturally diminish and which will need to be reduced.

One successful desktop publishing service owner, while in a busy period, decided that times would be much slower six months hence. So he talked with his bank and other creditors, offering to prepay debts and expenses, so he could cut back payments later. It worked. When times got rougher, he reduced his expenses and weathered the problem.

If you aren't into your slow season yet, you can also talk to your lender about building a line of credit now that will help you get through the tougher times ahead.

Another source for cash to tide you through a recession is a second mortgage on your building, your home, or other large asset. Speak with your lender about this opportunity. Even if you decide not to take out a second mortgage, you will be ready if and when you need to do so.

Finally, consider widening your market. Travel to a nearby metropolitan area and study whether you can expand your services to reach it. If so, you can pick up additional sales by either subcontracting your services or by promoting them in the expanded market. It certainly beats starving at home.

Advanced Expense Management Ideas

Every dollar saved in overhead is a dollar of net profit on the bottom line—and a dollar less borrowed.

The object of reducing costs in your desktop publishing business is to increase profits. Increasing profits through cost reduction must be based on the concept of an organized, planned program. Unless adequate records are maintained through an efficient and accurate accounting system, there can be no basis for analyzing costs.

Cost reduction is not simply attempting to slash any and all expenses without order. The owner-manager must understand the nature of expenses and how expenses interrelate with sales, inventories, overhead, gross profits, and net profits. Nor does cost reduction mean only the reduction of specific expenses. You can achieve greater profits through more efficient use of your expense dollar. Some of the ways you do this are by increasing the average sale per customer, by getting a larger return for your promotion and sales dollar, and by improving your internal methods and procedures.

As an example, one small desktop publisher was quite pleased when, in a single year, sales went from $60,000 to $155,000. However, at the end of the year, records showed that net profit the prior year, with lower sales, was actually higher than with increased sales. Why? Because the expenses of doing business grew at a rate faster than the income.

Your goal should be to pay the right price for prosperity. Determining that price for your operation goes beyond knowing what your expenses are. Reducing expenses to increase profit requires that you obtain the most efficient use of your expense dollars.

For example, checking job records, you might determine that one of your employees is significantly less efficient than other employees performing the same tasks. You can reduce expenses by increasing this employee's efficiency through training. Watching this employee perform the job, you can determine where the inefficiencies are and address them. If done with consideration, your employee will appreciate the advice, and so will your profit line.

Sometimes you cannot cut an expense item. But you can get more from it and thus increase your profits. In analyzing your expenses, you should use percentages rather than actual dollar amounts. For example, if you increase sales and keep the dollar amount of an expense the same, you have decreased that expense as a percentage of income. When you decrease your cost percentage, you increase your percentage of profit.

If your sales volume remains the same, you can also increase the percentage of profit by reducing a specific item of expense. Your goal, of course, is to do both—to decrease specific expenses and increase their productive worth at the same time.

Before you can determine whether cutting expenses will increase profits, you need information about your operation. This information can be obtained only if you have an adequate record-keeping system, as discussed earlier.

Your income statement provides a summary of expense information and is the focal point in locating expenses that can be cut. For this reason, the information should be as current as possible. If you prepare an income statement only at the end of the year, you should consider getting one more often. At the end of each quarter is usually sufficient for smaller firms. Larger desktop publishing services should receive the information on a monthly basis.

Regardless of the frequency, the best option is to prepare two income statements. One statement should report the sales, expenses, profit/loss of your operations cumulatively for the current business year to date. The other statement should report on the same items for the last complete month or quarter. Each of the statements should also carry the following information:

- Current year's figures and each item as a percentage of sales
- Previous year's figures and the percentages
- The difference between previous year and current year—over or under
- Budgeted figures and the respective percentages
- The difference between current year actuals and the budgeted figures—over or under
- Average percentages for similar businesses (available from trade associations and the U.S. Department of Labor)
- The difference between your annual percentages and the industry ratios—over or under

This information allows you to locate expense variations in three ways:

1. By comparing the current year to the previous year
2. By comparing expenses to your budgeted figures
3. By comparing your percentages to the operating ratios for similar businesses

The percentage figure is an important basis for comparison, representing a common denominator for all three methods. You should then study the dollar amounts to determine what kind of corrective action is needed.

Because your cost cutting will come largely from variable expenses, you should make sure that they are indicated on your income statements. Again, variable expenses fluctuate with the increase or decrease of sales volume. Examples include overtime pay, temporary help, advertising, salaries, commissions, payroll taxes.

When you have located a problem expense area, the next step obviously is to reduce that cost so as to increase your profit. A key to the effectiveness of your cost-cutting action is the worth of the various expenditures. As long as you know the worth of your expenditures, you can profit by making small improvements in expenses. Keep a sharp eye and an open mind. It is better to do a spot analysis once a month than to wait several months and then do a detailed study.

Decide on an action and take it as soon as possible. You can refine your cost-cutting action as you go along. Be persistent. Results typically come slower than you might like. Keep in mind that only persistent analysis of your records and constant action can prevent expenses from eating up profit.

How to Reduce Overhead

Business overhead is simply the costs of keeping your doors open. If your desktop publishing business is located in your home, overhead costs are probably small. But if you have an office and employees, your overhead is greater. It's also large if you have high debt to banks, suppliers, and backers.

The suggestion made earlier in this book was to start out small and let your growing business force you into larger quarters. That is, depending on your desktop publishing market, start with an office in a corner of your home. Then, as business grows, take on greater obligations for additional overhead. If you build a perception of quality in your customer's mind, you won't have to maintain impressive offices. Few customers will decide not to do business with you because your office is in your home.

You can also reduce overhead by carefully watching the costs of supplies. Printed stationery is an excellent way to promote the quality of your business, but you don't need printed notepads unless the customer will see them. It is inexpensive to purchase generic ink pens that include your business name and phone number. But don't buy so many that you have to throw them out because you've changed your address or phone number. Buy supplies in quantity if you can, but not more than you will use in three to six months unless you're certain that they won't become out-of-date.

Labor costs is one place where the profits of a small desktop publishing business can quickly be eaten away. Don't hire an office manager or secretary until you absolutely must. It's more profitable to do the required filing and office functions yourself after normal business hours or on weekends. Or you can ask the help of a spouse or older child who you can put on the payroll as soon as your business can afford it.

Some small desktop publishing services use temporary help or outside services rather than hiring employees and dealing with all the taxes and record-keeping required. They use a bookkeeping or accounting service, a janitorial service (or yourself), an answering service, and a secretarial service. These owners contract out work they can't handle to other desktop publishers. They know that the complexity of regulations and taxation is endlessly multiplied with the first employee hired—so they avoid hiring anyone until their success requires them to do so.

Long distance phone calls can quickly add to your expenses and cut into your profits—especially when they are personal calls made by employees. Many successful desktop publishing services use a telephone call record to keep track of long distance calls, then compare the report with the monthly phone bill. Calls not listed on the report are assumed to be personal calls and checked out.

An Eye to the Future

As your desktop publishing service grows, there are many new elements to your task of managing a successful business. You must consider and plan for the loss of a key person in the business structure. You must review you options if the business fails. Consider the long-term and begin planning for retirement. Planning well for tomorrow can reduce your worries today.

Succession in a Proprietorship

The personal skills, reputation, and management ability of the sole proprietor make the business successful. Without these human characteristics, the business is worth only the liquidation value of the tangible assets.

The sole proprietor's personal and business assets are one and the same. When death occurs, the loss can cause financial disaster to the proprietor's estate and to the business. The business that was producing a good living for the owner and family will become a defunct business. What are the options?

The business may be transferred to a capable family member as a gift through provisions in the proprietor's will or by a sale provided through a prearranged purchase agreement effective at death. Cash is needed to offset losses to the business caused by the owner's death, to equalize the value of bequests made to other family members if the transfer is a gift, and to provide funds if the transfer is through sale.

If the buyer is a key employee, competitor, or other person, the business may be transferred at death, based on a prearranged sale agreement. However, cash is needed to provide a business continuation fund to meet expenses and perhaps offset losses until the business adjusts to the new management.

If future management is not available, then the business must be liquidated. Cash is needed to offset the difference between the business's going-concern value and its auction-block liquidation value, to provide a fund for income replacement to the family, and to pay outstanding business debts.

Succession in a Partnership

Unless there is a written agreement to the contrary, the death of a partner automatically dissolves the firm. In the absence of such an agreement, surviving partners have no right to buy the deceased's partnership interest. Surviving partners cannot assume the goodwill or take over the assets without consent of the deceased's estate. If the deceased was in debt to the partnership, the estate must settle the account in full and in cash.

The surviving partners act as liquidating trustees. Under typical partnership agreements they have exclusive possession of firm property, but no right to carry on the business. If the business is continued, the surviving partners must share all profits with the deceased's estate and are liable for all losses. They must convert everything into cash at the best price obtainable. They must make an accounting to the deceased's estate and divide the proceeds with the estate. They must liquidate themselves out of their business and income.

What are the options a business has on the death of a partner? If the surviving partner and deceased's heirs do nothing, the business is liquidated, resulting in auction-price value for the salable assets. The business may receive nothing for goodwill. This is a disastrous solution for both the deceased partner's family and the surviving partners, terminating their jobs and those of employees.

The surviving partners may attempt to reorganize the partnership by taking the heirs into the partnership. But if heirs are incapable of working, the survivors must do all the work and share the profits. The surviving partners can also accept a new partner picked by the heirs. The surviving partners can also sell their interest in the business to the deceased partner's heirs, or conversely, buy out the heirs' interest.

Of course, partners can make preparations for a smoother reorganization after a death. Buy and sell agreements, funded with life insurance should be entered into while all partners are alive. Such an agreement, drafted by an attorney, will typically include a commitment by each partner not to dispose of his or her interest without first offering it at an agreed sale price to the partnership. The agreement will also include a provision for the partnership to buy a deceased partner's interest. The funding of the purchase will typically be from the proceeds of a life insurance policy written for that specific purpose.

Succession in a Corporation

After the death of a stockholder who has been active in the operation of a closely held corporation, the business entity continues its legal structure, but not its personal structure. The interests of the heirs of the deceased inevitably comes in conflict with the interests of the surviving associates.

What options are available to surviving stockholders? The deceased's family may retain the stock interest. If the heirs have a majority interest, they may choose to become personally involved in management. Or they may choose to remain inactive, elect a new board of directors and force the company to pay dividends. In either case, the surviving stockholders may lose a voice in management and possibly their jobs, while the deceased's family may become heirs to a business on the brink of failure. If the heirs have a minority interest and are not employed by the surviving associates, their only means of receiving an income from the corporation will be through dividends.

After the death of a stockholder, the deceased's heirs or estate may offer to sell the stock interest to the surviving stockholders. Or an outside buyer may be interested in purchasing stock in the corporation. While all of the interested parties are alive, they can enter into a binding buy and sell agreement funded with life insurance. A Stockholder's Buy and Sell Agreement, drawn up with the assistance of your corporate attorney and accountant, outlines the terms.

Death of Key Employees

Many growing firms develop key employees who represent assets the firm cannot afford to be without. Even though these key employees may not own an interest in the firm, they are nonetheless valuable to its continuation. So what happens if a key employee dies?

Desktop publishing services with key employees should consider life insurance payable to the firm upon their death or disability. How much life insurance? It should be an amount sufficient to offset financial losses during the readjustment period, to retain good credit standing, to assure customers and suppliers that the company will continue as usual. In addition, key-employee insurance can retire loans, mortgages, bonds, attract and train a successor, or carry out ongoing plans for expansion and new developments. Talk to your insurance agent about the appropriate policy for insuring your business against the loss of a proprietor, a partner, a stockholder, or a key employee. It's one of the costs of growth.

Smell the Roses

The primary reason your started your own business is to increase your opportunities to enjoy life. You wanted to offer a needed service; you wanted to help others; you wanted to extend your skills in desktop publishing and in business; you wanted to be able to afford the better things of life. However, you didn't want to spend your entire waking time working. In fact, you may get so caught up in the chase for success that you miss the opportunities that success brings along the way.

Those who have found success in the desktop publishing and other fields will tell you that it is often empty if not shared with others. And that doesn't mean waiting until a successful destination—say at $1 million net worth—is reached. It means sharing success with others along the way, on a day-to-day basis—with your close family, or a few good friends, or a charitable organization. In any case, consider that your financial success will mean much more to you if you can use it to bring physical, emotional, or spiritual success to others.

Manage your life outside your business as you do your time at the business. Look for ways of helping others. Find methods of giving yourself the things you most enjoy, whether time with friends, time with hobbies, time with competitive sports, time alone, or all of the above. Especially, take time to recharge your batteries. You will use lots of personal energy in starting, managing, and growing your desktop publishing business. Make sure you take the time to re-energize yourself.

When to Quit

The failure rate of new businesses is very high. It lowers as your desktop publishing service matures. The longer you're in business, the greater the chance that you will continue in business. However, your desktop publishing business can fail at any time. Most fail because they don't have a functioning record-keeping system, so they're not sure exactly when or how they fail, they just do. As has been emphasized, a key element of continued success is maintaining good records and learning how to manage by them.

But there may come a time when business conditions require that you throw in the towel. If you're not making sufficient profit or are reducing your capital to losses, you will soon be in financial trouble. What to do?

First, cut overhead as much as possible. The sooner this is done, the longer your business will survive—maybe long enough to find a solution.

Next, sell unused or inefficient assets. Of course, you must maintain your working tools. But maybe you can move your office to a less expensive location—even back home.

Then talk with your creditors about the situation and what you plan to do. Some may be very helpful in offering a workable solution—an extension of credit, assistance in finding additional contracts, or even purchase of stock in your business.

Finally, as necessary, talk with your attorney about your legal obligations and options. No one wants to declare bankruptcy, but it may be necessary. Or you may decide to set up a payment schedule for all debts and return to the work force as an employee.

There is no shame in failing to succeed—just in failing to try. You can use what you learned from the experience to increase your worth to an employer. Who better to manage a desktop publishing business than one who has learned what doesn't work.

Of course, now that you've planned out how to minimize losses, you probably won't have to. In fact, you look forward to retirement.

Planning to Retire

When should you retire from your profitable desktop publishing business? When you want to. Some desktop publishers will hold off retiring until they are no longer physically able to work their trade. Others make plans to retire when they are 65 or even 62 years of age. Still others give their business 10 or 20 years to grow, then sell it to semi-retire or to move to a different trade. Some work their children into it, then gradually turn it over to them.

Some successful desktop publishing service owners will sell their shares to a partner or to another corporation. Others will sell or give their equity in the business to a relative. Some will sell out to key employees or to competitors. A few will simply liquidate their assets and keep the proceeds.

The business can be sold outright for cash, earning the owner a cash settlement for their equity. Or the seller can "carry the paper" or sell it on a contract with a down payment and monthly payments for a specified term. In this case, buyers will often require the seller to sign a non-competition contract preventing the seller from working for a competing desktop publishing service or starting a similar business in the same market.

Action Guidelines

This is the end of the beginning. You now have many of the tools you need to start and succeed with your own desktop publishing service. Here's how you can put this final chapter into action:

- ✔ Apply the problem-solving techniques in this chapter to a current problem that your desktop publishing service is facing or expects to face.
- ✔ Even if you don't plan to hire anyone, review the methods of managing employees. If nothing else, it will remind you of why you don't want to increase your staff for a while.
- ✔ If you have or expect to hire employees, review the information on benefits programs to determine which best fit your business and philosophy.
- ✔ Find a local temporary employment office that may be able to help you during busy times.
- ✔ Consult with your insurance agent to make sure you are not undercovered nor overbilled.
- ✔ Plan today for how your business will survive the death of a principal, partner, or key employee.
- ✔ Periodically review your expenses to ensure you are getting the most from each dollar you spend.
- ✔ Have fun with your desktop publishing service and your life!

RESOURCES FOR SMALL BUSINESS

These publications on proven management techniques for small businesses are available from **Upstart Publishing Company, Inc.**, 12 Portland St., Dover, NH 03820. For a free current catalog, call (800) 235-8866 outside New Hampshire, or 749-5071 in state.

The Business Planning Guide, 6th edition, 1992, David H. Bangs, Jr. and Upstart Publishing Company, Inc. A manual that helps you write a business plan and financing proposal tailored to your business, your goals, and your resources. Includes worksheets and checklists. (Softcover, 208 pp., $19.95)

The Market Planning Guide, 4th edition, 1994, David H. Bangs, Jr. and Upstart Publishing Company, Inc. A manual to help small-business owners put together a goal-oriented, resource-based marketing plan with action steps, benchmarks and time lines. Includes worksheets and checklists to make implementation and review easier. (Softcover, 180 pp., $19.95)

The Cash Flow Control Guide, 1990, David H. Bangs, Jr. and Upstart Publishing Company, Inc. A manual to help small-business owners solve their number one financial problem. Includes worksheets and checklists. (Softcover, 88 pp., $14.95)

The Personnel Planning Guide, 1988, David H. Bangs, Jr. and Upstart Publishing Company, Inc. A 176-page manual outlining practical, proven personnel management techniques, including hiring, managing, evaluating and compensating personnel. Includes worksheets and checklists. (Softcover, 176 pp., $19.95)

The Start Up Guide: A One-Year Plan for Entrepreneurs, 2nd edition, 1994, David H. Bangs, Jr. and Upstart Publishing Company, Inc. This book utilizes the same step-by-step, no-jargon method as *The Business Planning Guide*, to help even those with no business training through the process of beginning a successful business. (Softcover, 176 pp., $19.95)

Managing By the Numbers: Financial Essentials for the Growing Business, 1992, David H. Bangs, Jr. and Upstart Publishing Company, Inc. Straightforward techniques for getting the maximum return with a minimum of detail in your business's financial management. (Softcover, 160 pp., $19.95.)

Building Wealth, 1992, David H. Bangs, Jr. and the editors of *Common Sense*. A collection of tested techniques designed to help you plan your personal finances and how to plan your business finances to benefit you, your family, and employees. (Softcover, 168 pp., $19.95)

Buy the Right Business—At the Right Price, 1990, Brian Knight and the Associates of Country Business, Inc. Many people who would like to be in business for themselves think strictly of starting a business. In some cases, buying a going concern may be preferable—and just as affordable. (Softcover, 152 pp., $18.95)

Borrowing for Your Business, 1991, George M. Dawson. This is a book for borrowers and about lenders. Includes detailed guidelines on how to select a bank and a banker, how to answer the lender's seven most important questions, how your banker looks at a loan, and how to get a loan renewed. (Hardcover, 160 pp., $19.95)

Can This Partnership Be Saved?, 1992, Peter Wylie and Mardy Grothe. The authors offer solutions and hope for problems between key people in business. (Softcover, 272 pp., $19.95)

Cases in Small Business Management, 1994, John Edward de Young. A compilation of intriguing and useful case studies in typical small business problems. (Softcover, 258 pp., $24.95)

The Complete Guide to Selling Your Business, 1992, Paul Sperry and Beatrice Mitchell. A step-by-step guide through the entire process from how to determine when the time is right to sell to negotiating the final terms. (Hardcover, 160 pp., $21.95)

The Complete Selling System, 1991, Pete Frye. This book can help any manager or salesperson, even those with no experience, find the solutions to some of the most common dilemmas in managing sales. (Hardcover, 192 pp., $21.95)

Creating Customers, 1992, David H. Bangs, Jr. and the editors of *Common Sense*. A book for business owners and managers who want a step-by-step approach to selling and promoting. Techniques include inexpensive market research, pricing your goods and services and writing a usable marketing plan. (Softcover, 176 pp., $19.95)

The Entrepreneur's Guide to Going Public, 1994, James B. Arkebauer with Ron Schultz. A comprehensive and useful book on a subject that is the ultimate dream of most entrepreneurs—making an initial public offering (IPO). (Softcover, 368 pp., $19.95)

Export Profits, 1992, Jack S. Wolf. This book shows how to find the right foreign markets for your product, cut through the red tape, minimize currency risks, and find the experts who can help. (Softcover, 304 pp., $19.95)

Financial Troubleshooting, 1992, David H. Bangs, Jr. and the editors of *Common Sense*. This book helps the owner/manager use basic diagnostic methods to monitor the health of the business and solve problems before damage occurs. (Softcover, 192 pp., $19.95)

Financial Essentials for Small Business Success, 1994, Joseph Tabet and Jeffrey Slater. Designed to show readers where to get the information they need and how planning and recordkeeping will enhance the health of any small business. (Softcover, 272 pp., $19.95)

From Kitchen to Market, 1992, Stephen Hall. A practical approach to turning culinary skills into a profitable business. (Softcover, 208 pp., $24.95)

The Home-Based Entrepreneur, 1993, Linda Pinson and Jerry Jinnett. A step-by-step guide to all the issues surrounding starting a home-based business. Issues such as zoning, labor laws, and licensing are discussed and forms are provided to get you on your way. (Softcover, 192 pp. $19.95)

Keeping the Books, 1993, Linda Pinson and Jerry Jinnett. Basic business recordkeeping both explained and illustrated. Designed to give you a clear understanding of small business accounting by taking you step-by-step through general records, development of financial statements, tax reporting, scheduling, and financial statement analysis. (Softcover, 208 pp., $19.95)

The Language of Small Business, 1994, Carl O. Trautmann. A clear, concise dictionary of small business terms for students and small business owners. (Softcover, 416 pp., $19.95)

Marketing Your Invention, 1992, Thomas Mosley. This book dispels the myths and clearly communicates what inventors need to know to successfully bring their inventions to market. (Softcover, 232 pp., $19.95)

100 Best Retirement Businesses, 1994, Lisa Angowski Rogak with David H. Bangs, Jr. A one-of-a-kind book bringing retirees the inside information on the most interesting and most lucrative businesses for them. (Softcover, 416 pp., $15.95)

The Small Business Computer Book, 1993, Robert Moskowitz. This book does not recommend particular systems, but rather provides readers with a way to think about these choices and make the right decisions for their businesses. (Softcover, 190 pp., $19.95)

Start Your Own Business for $1,000 or Less, 1994, Will Davis. Shows readers how to get started in the "mini-business" of their dreams with less than $1,000. (Softcover, 280 pp., $17.95)

Steps to Small Business Start-Up, 1993, Linda Pinson and Jerry Jinnett. A step-by-step guide for starting and succeeding with a small or home-based business. Takes you through the mechanics of business start-up and gives an overview of information on such topics as copyrights, trademarks, legal structures, recordkeeping, and marketing. (Softcover, 256 pp., $19.95)

Target Marketing for the Small Business, 1993, Linda Pinson and Jerry Jinnett. A comprehensive guide to marketing your business. This book not only shows you how to reach your customers, it also gives you a wealth of information on how to research that market through the use of library resources, questionnaires, demographics, etc. (Softcover, 176 pp., $19.95)

On Your Own: A Woman's Guide to Starting Your Own Business, 2nd edition, 1993, Laurie Zuckerman. *On Your Own* is for women who want hands-on, practical information about starting and running their own business. It deals honestly with issues like finding time for your business when you're also the primary care provider, societal biases against women and credit discrimination. (Softcover, 320 pp., $19.95)

Problem Employees, 1991, Dr. Peter Wylie and Dr. Mardy Grothe. Provides managers and supervisors with a simple, practical and straightforward approach to help all employees, especially problem employees, significantly improve their work performance. (Softcover, 272 pp., $22.95)

Problems and Solutions in Small Business Management, 1994, the editors of *Forum*, the journal of the Association of Small Business Development Centers. A collection of case studies selected from the pages of *Forum* magazine. (Softcover, 200 pp., $21.95)

The Restaurant Planning Guide, 1992, Peter Rainsford and David H. Bangs, Jr. This book takes the practical techniques of *The Business Planning Guide* and combines it with the expertise of Peter Rainsford, a restaurateur and a professor at the Cornell School of Hotel Administration. Topics include: establishing menu prices, staffing and scheduling, controlling costs and niche marketing. (Softcover, 176 pp., $19.95)

Successful Retailing, 2nd edition, 1993, Paula Wardell. Provides hands-on help for those who want to start or expand their retail business. Sections include: strategic planning, marketing and market research and inventory control. (Softcover, 176 pp., $19.95)

The Upstart Guide to Owning and Managing an Antiques Business, 1994, Lisa Angowski Rogak. Provides the information a prospective antiques dealer needs to run a business profitably. (Softcover, 224 pp., $15.95)

The Upstart Guide to Owning and Managing a Bar or Tavern, 1994, Roy Alonzo. Provides essential information on planning, making the initial investment, financial management, and marketing a bar or tavern. (Softcover, 256 pp., $15.95)

The Upstart Guide to Owning and Managing a Bed & Breakfast, 1995, Lisa Angowski Rogak. Provides information on choosing the best location, licensing and what really goes on behind the scenes. (Softcover, 224 pp., $15.95)

The Upstart Guide to Owning and Managing a Résumé Service, 1995, Dan Ramsey. Shows how any reader can turn personnel, writing, and computer skills into a lucrative resume-writing business. (Softcover, 224 pp., $15.95)

The Woman Entrepreneur, 1992, Linda Pinson and Jerry Jinnett. Thirty-three successful women business owners share their practical ideas for success and their sources for inspiration. (Softcover, 244 pp., $14.00)

Other Available Titles

The Complete Guide to Business Agreements, 1993, Ted Nicholas, Enterprise • Dearborn. Contains 127 of the most commonly needed business agreements. (Loose-leaf binder, $69.95)

The Complete Small Business Legal Guide, 1993, Robert Friedman, Enterprise • Dearborn. Provides the hands-on help you need to start a business, maintain all necessary records, properly hire and fire employees, and deal with the many changes a business goes through. (Softcover, $69.95)

Forecasting Sales and Planning Profits: A No-Nonsense Guide for Growing a Business, 1986, Kenneth E. Marino, Probus Publishing Co. Concise and easily applied forecasting system, based on an analysis of market potential and sale requirements, to help establish the basis for financial statements in your business plan. Book is currently out-of-print, check second-hand bookstores for the title.

Guerrilla Marketing: Secrets for Making Big Profits from Your Small Business, 1984, J. Conrad Levinson, Houghton-Mifflin. A classic tool kit for small businesses. (Hardcover, 226 pp., $14.95)

How to Form Your Own Corporation Without a Lawyer for Under $75.00, 1992, Ted Nicholas, Enterprise • Dearborn. A good book for helping you to discover all the unique advantages of incorporating while at the same time learning how quick, easy, and inexpensive the process can be. (Softcover, $19.95)

Marketing Sourcebook for Small Business, 1989, Jeffrey P. Davidson, John Wylie Publishing. A good introductory book for small business owners with excellent definitions of important marketing terms and concepts. (Hardcover, 325 pp., $24.95)

The Small Business Survival Kit: 101 Troubleshooting Tips for Success, 1993, John Ventura, Enterprise • Dearborn. Offers compassionate insight into the emotional side of financial difficulties as well as a nuts-and-bolts consideration of options for the small businessperson experiencing tough times. (Softcover, $19.95)

INDEX

A

Accountant, hiring of, 74-76, 78
Accounts payable, 86, 133-136; receivable, 86, 89-90, 134-136
Action guidelines, 14, 41, 55, 78, 109, 131, 153, 187
Advertising, first years, 11-12; newspapers, publishing of, 1-2, 4; print, 113, 125-126; programs, establishment of, 118-122
Alternative services, 13
American Institute of Graphic Arts, 46
Answering service, 12
Art programs, 29
Artistic skills, 9
Assets, understanding of, 88
Association for the Development of Electronic Publishing Technique, 45-46
Attorneys, 73-74, 78
Awards, 125

B

Balance sheet, 137
Banks, publishing newsletters for, 2-3

Benefit plans. *See* Employee benefit plans
Books. *See* Reference books
Brochures, 1-5, 6, 29
Budget, fine tuning, 12; operating, 81-83, 109
Business, cards, 1, 4, 6, 29; cycles, 174-175; day, example of, 5-6; failure, 185-186; knowledge, fundamentals of, 7; name, selection of, 59-61; new, package for, 6; paperless, 7; plan, 4, 58-59, 78; problem solving, 155-160; structures, 67-73, 78; success, 155-187

C

Capital, operating, 13
Cash, and accrual accounting, 88-89; flow, forecasts, 137-142; flow, requirements, 75
Catalogs, publishing of, 4
Collateral loan, 145-146
Competition, 14
Computer, aided publishing (CAP), 3; introduction to, 7, 20-38, 41
Conventions, 43, 46
Copiers, 35-36

Corporation, succession in, 182-183
Corporations. See Incorporating
Cosigner loans, 144-145
Cost reduction, 175-180
Costs, operating, 39-40, 79-81, 109
Credit, cards, 144, 149, 153; development of, 142
Customer, credit, 149; interview, 44-45; prospective, 43, 55, 111-117, 131; understanding of, 114-116

D

Databases, 30-31
Defining client needs, 8
Design skills, 9, 15
Desktop publishing, markets for, 3, 6-7; opportunities for, 1-14
Digital cameras, 37-38
Direct expenses, 9-10
Directions, publishing of, 1, 5
Directories, publishing of, 4
Disabilities Act (ADA), 65
Diskettes, 23-24
Document processors, 27-28
Documents, production of, 7-8

E

Electronic files, 7
Employee benefit plans, 162-167, 187
Employees, hiring of, 10, 104-106; loss of, 183-184, 187; managing of, 161, 187; manuals, publishing of, 4; temporary, 167-169, 179-180
Employment laws, 66-67
Equipment, leasing, 145; records, 86, 91-92, 109
Estimating costs, 3
Expenses, direct, 9-10; fixed and variable, 40; reduction of, 12

F

Family, as employees, 12; owned business, 2-3
Fax machines, 2, 36-37
Fees. See Pricing
Financial, goals, assessment of, 18-19; planning, improvement of, 149-153; requirements, 38-41; worksheet, 39
First business year estimates, 10-11
Flyers, publishing of, 4
Franchises, 49-50, 55
Furniture, 20
Future, of desktop publishing services, 7; planning, 180-187

G

Goals, personal assessment of, 15-16, 41
Governmental offices, 43, 55

H

Helping others, 15-16. See also Goals, Values
Hiring. See Employees
History books, local publishing of, 4

Hourly rates, 2-3, 9. *See also* Pricing
How to Make $100,000 a Year in Desktop Publishing, 4

I

Income, potential, 9-12; statement, 136
Incorporating, 2-3, 72-73
Instructions, publishing of, 1, 5
Insurance, 13, 170-174; "electronic," 25; agent, 77, 78, 187; benefits, employees. *See* Employee benefit plans
Integrated programs, 31-32
Interest rates, 146-147
International Franchise Association (IFA), 49-50
Inventory, 86
IRS, 106-108, 109

J

Journals, 85-86

L

Labor. *See* Employees
Laser printer, 20
Laws, employment, 66-67, 78; zoning, 65
Leases, 13
Letterhead, 1, 6
Liabilities, understanding, 88
Line of Credit, 144
Loans, types of, 143-146
Local business consultants, 6
Local publications/guides, publishing of, 3-4, 5
Location, 61-65, 78

M

Mailing labels, 6, 29
Market niches, 5, 111-113, 131
Marketing, 111-131
Medical offices, newsletters for, 6
Money management, 133-136
Motto, business, 60, 78

N

Naming business, 59-61
National Association for Desktop Publishers (ADTP), 4, 20,28, 33, 45
National Association of Secretarial Services (NASS), 46
National Composition and Prepress Association, 46
Net profit margin, 152
Net worth, understanding, 88
Newsletters, client, 8, 25; customer, publishing of, 2-4, 5, 6
Newspapers, publishing of, 4
Notebook, idea, 14

O

Office, equipment, 20-38; home, 12, 62, 103; hours, 5; location, 61-65, 78; shared, 63
On-line services, 48-49
Operating, budget, 81-83, 109; costs, 39-40, 79-81, 109; systems, 26-27
Operations, day to day, 79-109
Overhead, expenses, 9-11, 40; reduction, 178-180

P

Packages, for new business, 6
Paper, 6, 7, 13, 20, 38, 179; suppliers, 50-51
Partnership, 69-72; succession in, 181-182
Payroll, 86, 109; records, 90
Personalized folder, for new business, 6
Petty cash, 91
Plan of action, designing, 159-160
Postcard announcements, 6
Potential income, calculating, 6-14
Presentation documents, publishing of, 2-3, 5
Press release samples, 123-124
Pricing, 45, 92-100, 109; guide, example of, 95
Pricing Guide for Desktop Publishing, 94, 95, 96-97
Printed documents, experience with, 7, 43-44
Printers, 34-35, 41
Printing Industries of America, 46
Problem solving, 155-160, 187
Product, literature, 6; suppliers, 51
Production system, establishment of, 3, 7-8
Professional, offices, newsletters for, 6; trade associations, 43, 45-46, 55, 125
Profit potential, 9-12
Project cost estimating form, 96
Promotional documents, printing of, 2-3, 5
Proposals for new business, 6
Proprietorship, 2-3, 67-69; succession in, 180-181
Prospects, 111-117, 131

R

Ratio analysis, 150-152
Real estate guides, publishing of, 4
Record systems, understanding of, 86-92, 109
Recordkeeping, 74-76, 83-92, 109, 176-177
Reference books, for desktop publishing business, 43, 46-47, 49-50, 55; for small business, 189-196
Referral business, 10, 129-130, 131. *See also* Word-of-mouth
Regional publications, publishing of, 3-4, 5
Rent, 12-13
Repeat business, 10, 128-129
Resources, for desktop publishing service, 43-55; for small business, 189-196
Retail shop location, 12. *See also* Location
Retirement planning, 164-167, 186
Risk, insuring against, 171-174, 184; management, 12-14, 169-171; tolerance, assessment of, 19, 41

S

Salary, 9-12. *See also* Employees
Sales, calls, 5, 117-119, 171; documents, 6
Scanners, 24-25
Scholarship, establishment of, 125
Second business year estimates, 10
Selling your business, 186
Seminars, 43, 55
Service Corps of Retired Executives (SCORE), 52
Shopping mall location, 64. *See also* Location
Short-document service, 112
Slogans, business, 60, 78
Small Business Administration (SBA), loans, 147-149; resources, 51-53, 55
Software, 7, 20, 26-32, 41, 117
Solutions to client's problem, 8
Specializing, 5, 111-113, 125
Spreadsheets, 30
Standard industrial classification code, 61
Start-up, 57-78; costs, 39-40
Statement of purpose, 59, 78
Success, planning for, 58-59

T

Target market, 10
Task management, 100-102
Tax information resources, 53-54, 55
Taxes, payment of, 106-109
Technical documents, publishing of, 4, 6
Technology, keeping current with, 7
Telephone, marketing, 117-118; script, 119, 131
Temporary help, 167-169, 179-180, 187. *See also* Employees
Testimonials, 121-122, 131; sheet, example of, 101
Toll free number, 5
Tourism guides, publishing of, 3-4
Trade, associations. *See* Professional trade associations; journals, 43, 48, 50, 55
Training courses, 43, 46, 55
Typographers International Association, 46

V

Value vs. price, 98-99, 109
Values, personal assessment of, 17-18, 41

W

Word-of-mouth, 121-122
Working capital, 151-152
Writers, working with, 2-3

Y

Yellow pages advertising, 14, 120-121, 126-128, 131

Z

Zoning laws, 65